Be Strong & Be Brave...
for the Lord your God is with you.
Deuteronomy 31:6

By
Kristie Kerr & Paula Yarnes
with
Jeff Kerr & Aaron Broberg

Copyright 2015 Kristie Kerr and Paula Yarnes. All Rights Reserved.

No part of this book may be reproduced, transmitted, or utilized in any form or by any means, graphic, electronic or mechanical, including photocopying, recording, taping, or by any information storage or retrieval, without the permission in writing from the publisher.

Unless otherwise indicated, all Scripture quotations are taken from the Holy Bible, New Living Translation, copyright ©1996, 2004, 2007 by Tyndale House Foundation. Used by permission of Tyndale House Publishers, Inc., Carol Stream, Illinois 60188. All rights reserved.

THE HOLY BIBLE, NEW INTERNATIONAL VERSION®, NIV® Copyright © 1973, 1978, 1984, 2011 by Biblica, Inc.™ Used by permission. All rights reserved worldwide.

Scripture taken from The Message. Copyright ©1993, 1994, 1995, 1996, 2000, 2001, 2002. Used by permission of NavPress Publishing Group.

Scripture taken from the Contemporary English Version ©1991, 1992, 1995 by American Bible Society, Used by Permission.

Scripture taken from the Common English Bible P.O. Box 801 201 Eighth Avenue South Nashville, TN 37202-0801

Scripture taken from the International Standard Version Release 2.1. Copyright ©1996–2012 the ISV Foundation. All rights reserved internationally.

Scripture taken from the Holy Bible, NEW INTERNATIONAL READER'S VERSION®. Copyright © 1996, 1998 Biblica. All rights reserved throughout the world. Used by permission of Biblica.

ISBN: 978-0-9970676-1-3

Printed in the United States of America

1st Printing

CONTENTS

Just Be You 1-15
    Lesson 2
    Doodle Page 8
    Activity Sheet .9
    Bazooka Breakdown 12
    Bazooka Project 15

My True Reflection 17-29
    Lesson 18
    Doodle Page 24
    Activity Sheet .25
    Bazooka Breakdown 30
    Bazooka Project 33

Whatever 41-56
    Lesson 42
    Doodle Page 49
    Activity Sheet .51
    Bazooka Breakdown 53
    Bazooka Project 55

Every-Body 57-80
    Lesson 58
    Doodle Page 64
    Activity Sheet .65
    Bazooka Breakdown 71
    Bazooka Project 75

Why Am I Here 81-98
    Lesson 82
    Doodle Page 87
    Activity Sheet .89
    Bazooka Breakdown 94
    Bazooka Project 97

God Confidence 99-116
    Lesson 100
    Doodle Page .107
    Activity Sheet 109
    Bazooka Breakdown 111
    Bazooka Project 115

So Much Stuff 117-132
    Lesson 118
    Doodle Page .125
    Activity Sheet 127
    Bazooka Breakdown 129
    Bazooka Project 131

Courage 133-153
    Lesson 134
    Doodle Page .141
    Activity Sheet 143
    Bazooka Breakdown 146
    Bazooka Project 149

Dedicated to the boys who inspire us:

To Charlie whose tender heart and quiet spirit
remind us that **STRENGTH ISN'T ALWAYS LOUD**.

To Hunter who is **TENACIOUS AND KIND**...
and came up with the name Bazooka Boys.

To Chase who **LOVES UNCONDITIONALLY**.

To Reed who lit his homework on fire...
and then became an **HONOR STUDENT**.

To Jacob, the boy with the sensitive heart,
that captures people with his **LOVE FOR JUSTICE AND ALL THINGS SILLY**.

To Levi whose **DETERMINATION COULD DEMOLISH MOUNTAINS**
& smile could melt away the debris

To Zach who is a **TRUSTWORTHY, CONFIDENT, KIND-HEARTED** young man,
and NEVER forgets to kiss his mom goodnight!

To Li who is **KIND AND LOVING** and **ALWAYS** follows the rules!

To Stewart. The **TWINKLE IN YOUR EYE** and the tenderness in your heart
remind us that God really does make dreams come true.

You amaze us.
Go change the world.

Bazooka Boys ★ Who Am I?

JUST BE YOU

What's the Point?
God made you just the way you are...and you should be you!.

THEME VERSE:
For we are God's masterpiece.
Ephesians 2:10

RELATED BIBLE PASSAGE:
Psalm 139

Being a boy is awesome. It's so cool how we're all boys, but we're all so different. Some of us love to play sports. Some of us love to be outside whenever we can. Some of us love to play video games. Some of us play a musical instrument. And some of us love to do all of those things!

God made us all boys, yet He made us all so different. We're the same in a whole lot of ways, but we're different in a whole lot of ways, too!

The Bible tells us that God made each one of us.

"For You created my inmost being; You knit me together in my mother's womb."
—Psalm 139:13

EACH AND EVERY THING ABOUT YOU WAS HANDPICKED BY GOD.

I heard about this super cool store where you can make remote control race cars. You pick out the body of the car and then choose all the cool details. You can pick wheels, decals, and all kinds of different accessories to make your car 100% unique. Every combination is different because it's handpicked by the person creating it!

Or how about playing with LEGOs? The best part about playing with LEGOs is how many different pieces there are. There's no end to the different things you can make! You have pieces of all different shapes sizes and colors. You can build cars with wheels, boats with sails, planes with propellers, spaceships with wings, or some super awesome combination of all of those. LEGO creations are totally unique because each piece is handpicked by the person creating it! And when you make something original and super cool, you feel pretty good about it.

Bazooka Boys ★ Who Am I?

It was the same way when God created you! He picked out every single detail about you. He picked the color of your hair and the size of your ears. He decided which sports you would love or what instrument you would play with great skill. He determined the things you would be good at and the stuff you would love to do. There's **NOTHING** about you that wasn't handpicked by God when He created you!

"FOR WE ARE GOD'S MASTERPIECE. HE HAS CREATED US ANEW IN CHRIST JESUS, SO WE CAN DO THE GOOD THINGS HE PLANNED OF RUS LONG AGO."
—EPHESIANS 2:10

The Bible tells us that God was SO happy when He made you! He had created a lot of things, but creating YOU was the best thing He had ever done.

"For we are God's masterpiece. He has created us anew in Christ Jesus, so we can do the good things He planned for us long ago." —Ephesians 2:10

God only made **ONE** you. There's **NO** one else with the amazing combination of looks, personality, and talents that you have. You are one of a kind. You are very special.

Sometimes I wonder why God didn't just make us all the same. Have you every thought about that? Why didn't He just make one person and then make another one exactly the same, and then another one exactly the same?

But He didn't! He made each one of us unique and different.

The Bible tells us that God is **CREATIVE!** Actually, He's called the Creator! To be creative means to use lots of variety and imagination to make something really special. And that's exactly what God did when He made us. He used lots of uniqueness and differences to make us all so special and different.

Do you use just one crayon when you're drawing a picture? I mean, it would be a lot easier. You wouldn't have to spend time trying to decide which color to use. And then all your pictures would look the same. It would be very neat and orderly, right?!

I don't know about you, but when I draw a picture, I like to use ALL the colors! I love to use red and orange to make an explosion. I use black for the wheels on a truck. I use brown for the big mud puddle I'm about to drive through. I use bright colors for my favorite video game character.

When God made us, He used every color in the box. He didn't make us all orange. He didn't make us all purple. He didn't even make us all plain old green. He made us with an amazing combination of colors. He didn't make just one boy and then duplicate him over and over again. He made you special and original. You are a masterpiece!

So **WHY** do we spend **SO** much time trying to **LOOK** and **ACT** and **BE** just like everybody else? We try to be just like the "cool" kids at school. Or we think we should be just like our big brother. Or we try and look like athletes we see on TV or in magazines. Sometimes we feel bad about ourselves because we're different.

Can I tell you a secret? It's a really big one. Ready?

You **ARE** different.

Yup. No way of getting around it. You're different. You're not like everybody else. There's not a person on the planet like you.

We **KNOW** that God made us each different and original, right? So why should we feel bad about that? Why should we try and change something God planned? Why should we feel like we should be something other than **EXACTLY** who God made us to be?

I know other people can put a lot of pressure on us to be just like everyone else. Sometimes we feel like our differences make us stand out and we really just want to blend in. We can be picked on or left out because our differences, and that can be really hard.

But you know what? If you stop worrying about who other people want you to be and simply accept who God made you to be, you'll feel so much better! God doesn't **EVER** make mistakes. And He didn't make ANY mistakes when He made you.

When God created you, He was doing it for a reason. You see, God knows everything about you. And God knows everything you are ever going to do with

Bazooka Boys ★ Who Am I?

your life. Psalm 139:16 says "You saw me before I was born. Every day of my life was recorded in Your book. Every moment was laid out before a single day had passed."

God picked all the unique things about you so you could do **ALL** the things He wants you to do with your life. He gave you everything you need.

It's like this: if you were going to a friend's house to sleep over, you would pack your bag and make sure you had everything you needed for the next day or two. You'd make sure you had pajamas and your toothbrush, clothes for the next day, and hopefully some clean underwear! You would think about all the things you might need and pack them in your bag so you would have them when you needed them.

God packed your bag perfectly. He gave you everything you would need for your entire life when He created you. There's NOTHING about you that was an accident. You were carefully and purposefully created to do all the things God has planned for you!

Maybe God's plan for your life will have you teaching kids in another country, so He made you with a love for learning. He gave you a desire to travel and made you curious about other nations. He made you like different kinds of food and big hairy spiders. He gave you an ability to help others understand stuff they're studying. See? Everything about you is a part of God's plan. **THERE ARE NO ACCIDENTS OR MISTAKES.**

Instead of feeling bad about the things that make you different, start asking God to show you **WHY** He made you the way He did. I bet if you start focusing on the cool reasons God made you the way you are, you'll feel better and better about the things that make

KA-BOOM!!!

you stand out from other people. You'll start to get excited about the things that make you original because they're part of the incredibly awesome plan God has for you!

Johnny wasn't very good at sports. Actually, he stunk. He dreaded gym time at school because he was always picked last for teams and that made him feel bad. The boys would pick on him because he couldn't do a basketball layup. In the summer, all the boys in his class would play soccer together and spend lots of time having fun at practices and games, but Johnny was left out because he wasn't good enough to play on their soccer teams. He always felt like he didn't fit in.

But oh, how he loved to draw! He could spend hours with his sketch book making up characters and putting colors and designs together. Drawing came so easily, and whenever he got the chance to create a new picture, he jumped at it.

One day, the boys on the soccer team came to him. They wanted to design T-shirts for their team to help raise money for some tournaments. They wanted to come up with a really cool idea. They asked Johnny if he could draw a picture the team could put on their shirts.

What does it mean to be a masterpiece?

A masterpiece is a special creation of the creator. In some versions of the Bible, masterpiece is translated as "workmanship." We're God's workmanship. The Greek word for workmanship is "poiema." Do you ever wonder where we got the word "poem"? The Greek word "poiema" simply means "that which is made," "creation," or "a work of art." Did you know you're a work of art?

Johnny was SO excited. He came up with some fun ideas and showed the boys the next day. They loved it! They ended up using a few of his drawings to make sweatshirts and coffee mugs, too!

Bazooka Boys ★ Who Am I?

WEEK 1

This experience was HUGE for Johnny. He realized it was okay if he wasn't good at soccer because he was good at other things. He didn't need to be like everybody else, he just needed to be himself! God had made him good at art, so he should work as hard as he could on that and not worry about the things he **WASN'T** good at.

Johnny still got picked last in gym class, but it didn't matter as much as it used to. He knew God had given him a special gift, and it didn't matter if he wasn't good at sports.

YOU ARE ORIGINAL. YOU ARE DIFFERENT. AND YOU ARE EXACTLY WHO GOD CREATED YOU TO BE.

Closing Prayer: Dear God, Thank you for creating me. I know You made me unique and different for a purpose. I am so grateful that You handpicked everything about me. Help me to be okay with who You made me to be and not feel bad about the things that make me different. I love you. Amen.

DOODLE PAGE

YOU ARE A UNIQUE SUPERHERO!

Give yourself a superhero name and write out your superhero abilities. Make sure you draw your superhero logo on the cape and color it in!

I am a Masterpiece!

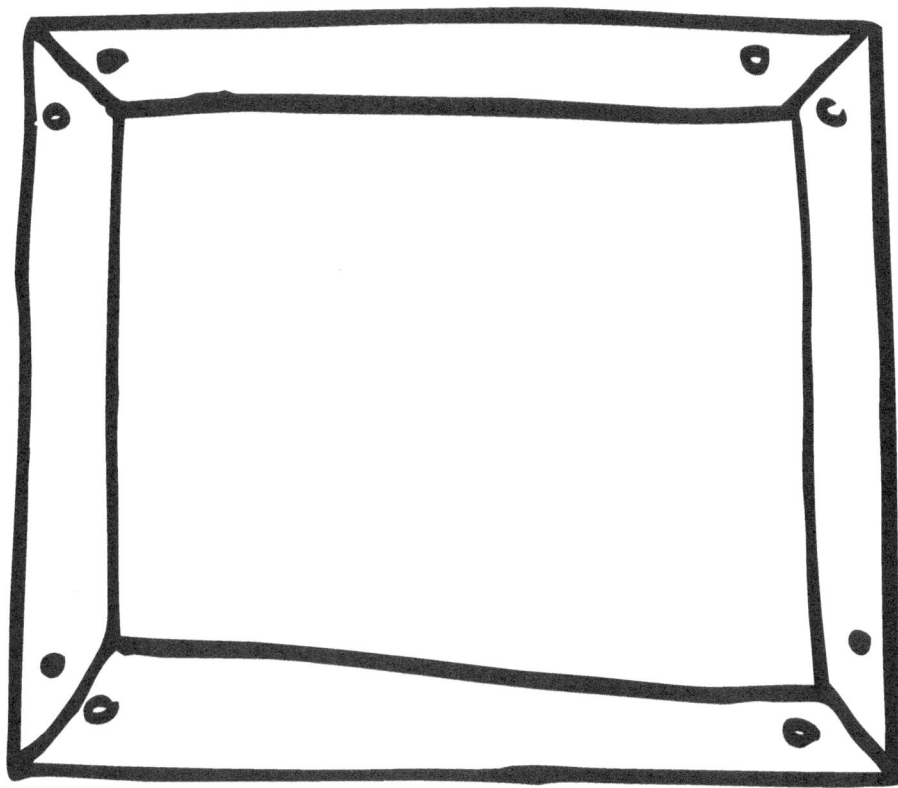

My name _____ My age _____

God made my eyes this color _____

God made my hair this color _____

My favorite sport _____

My favorite food _____

The special gifts God gave me (what I'm good at) are _____
_____

When I grow up I want to be_____

9

Read Psalm 139 (NIV), fill in the blanks, and find the missing words in the word search.

[1] You have _____ me, LORD, and You know me. [2] You know when I sit and when I rise; You perceive my _____ from afar. [3] You discern my going out and my lying down; You are _____ with all my ways. [4] Before a word is on my _____ You, LORD, know it completely. [5] You _____ me in behind and before, and You lay Your hand upon me. [6] Such knowledge is too _____ for me, too lofty for me to attain. [7] Where can I go from Your _____? Where can I flee from Your presence? [8] If I go up to the _____, You are there; if I make my bed in the depths, You are there. [9] If I rise on the _____ of the dawn, if I settle on the far side of the sea, [10] even there Your hand will _____ me, Your right hand will hold me fast. [11] If I say, "Surely the _____ will hide me and the light become night around me," [12] even the darkness will not be dark to You; the night will shine like the day, for darkness is as _____ to You. [13] For You created my inmost being; You _____ me together in my mother's womb. [14] I praise You because I am fearfully and _____ made; Your works are wonderful, I know that full well. [15] My frame was not hidden from You when I was made in the _____ place, when I was woven together in the depths of the earth. [16] Your eyes saw my unformed body; all the days ordained for me were _____ in Your book before one of them came to be. [17] How _____ to me are Your thoughts, God! How vast is the sum of them! [18] Were I to count them, they would outnumber the _____ of sand—when I awake, I am still with You.

Bazooka Boys ★ Who Am I?

WEEK 1

Word Search Puzzle

```
N M W R N T X S X G X E Y A E
S O F O I E T G Z N V U F D G
G X I R N H T Y K E Q G D V I
F R I L G D Y T R N D N E E P
N P A U L D E L I O I O H R R
S J O I H E A R T R T T C S E
G H H U N S B R F N W W R A C
T C E X T S Z E K U I X A R I
F A M I L I A R R N L H E I O
T S N E V A E H G W E L S E U
N G E D I U G S N I T S Y S S
U V G S E C R E T C S H S G G
O T H K B P C K H K S T G L F
C X Q U F W A C L E Z J A I Y
L U F R E D N O W D Y I D A L
```

WORD LIST

searched   *wonderful*   *darkness*   *written*
thoughts   *spirit*   *light*   *precious*
familiar   *heavens*   *knit*   *grains*
tongue   *wings*   *wonderfully*
hem   *guide*   *secret*

11

What is the coolest thing you've ever made? Draw a picture of it here, or describe it down to the very last detail!

God made each and every one of us. He created each one of us completely unique and different. What are some things that are unique about you? On the picture on the next page, draw in some of the things that you are good at. Add as many as you can think of!

Bazooka Boys ★ Who Am I?

WEEK 1

Write out this verse three times and see if you can memorize it!

For we are God's masterpiece. —Ephesians 2:10

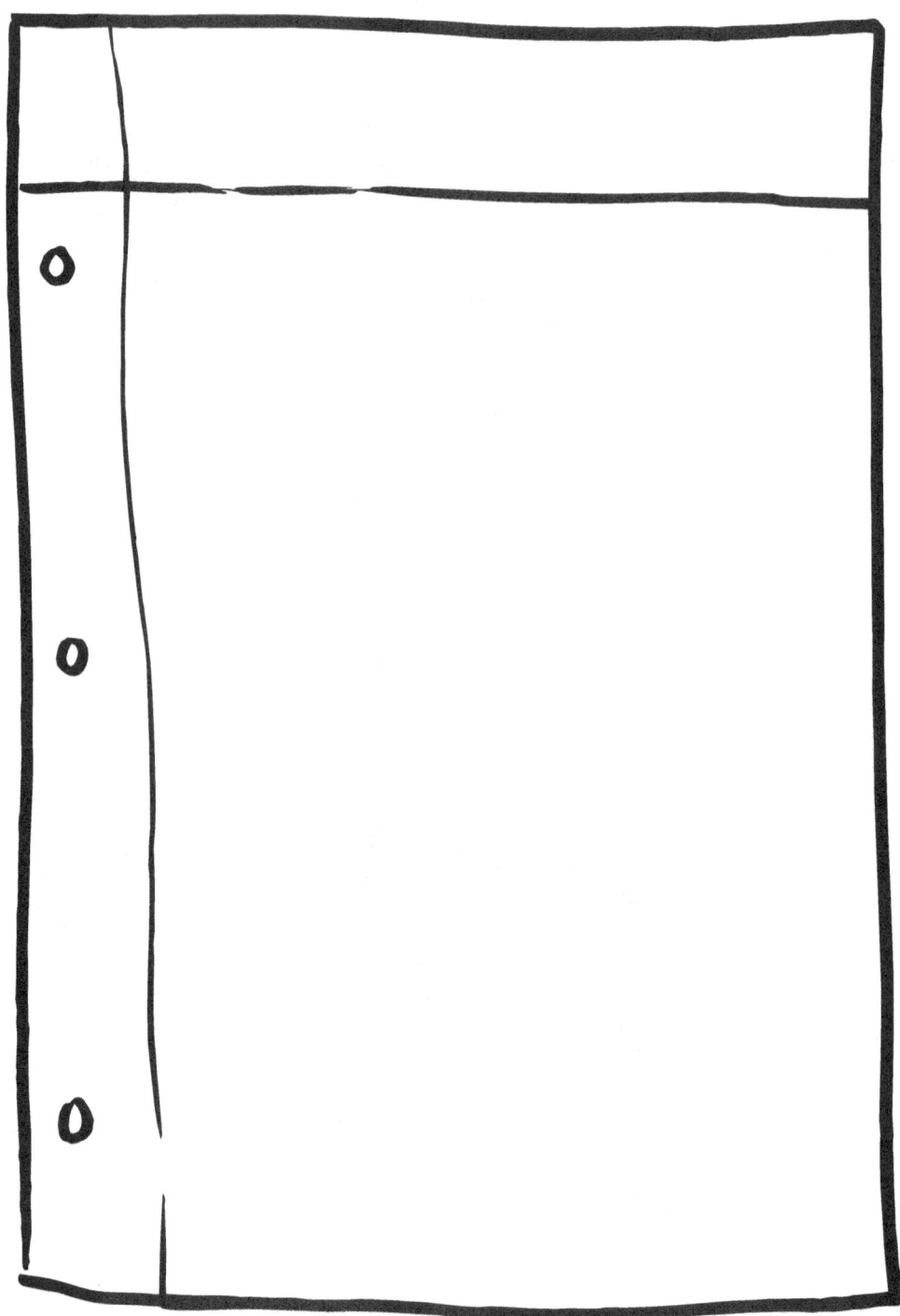

Bazooka Boys ★ Who Am I?

OPTION 1: LEGO SELF-PORTRAIT

Supplies

- Template found on page 16
- Crayons/Markers

Directions

- Make a LEGO self-portrait that shows something unique about your life and/or personality.

OPTION 2: LEGO CAR

Supplies

- LEGOs
- LEGO wheels
- Balloons
- Timer

Directions

1. Create a unique mini LEGO vehicle.

2. Attach a balloon by placing part of it (not the end) between two pieces of the LEGO car. Make sure the balloon opening isn't squished so air can flow freely.

3. Blow up the balloon, let go, and watch the LEGO car go!

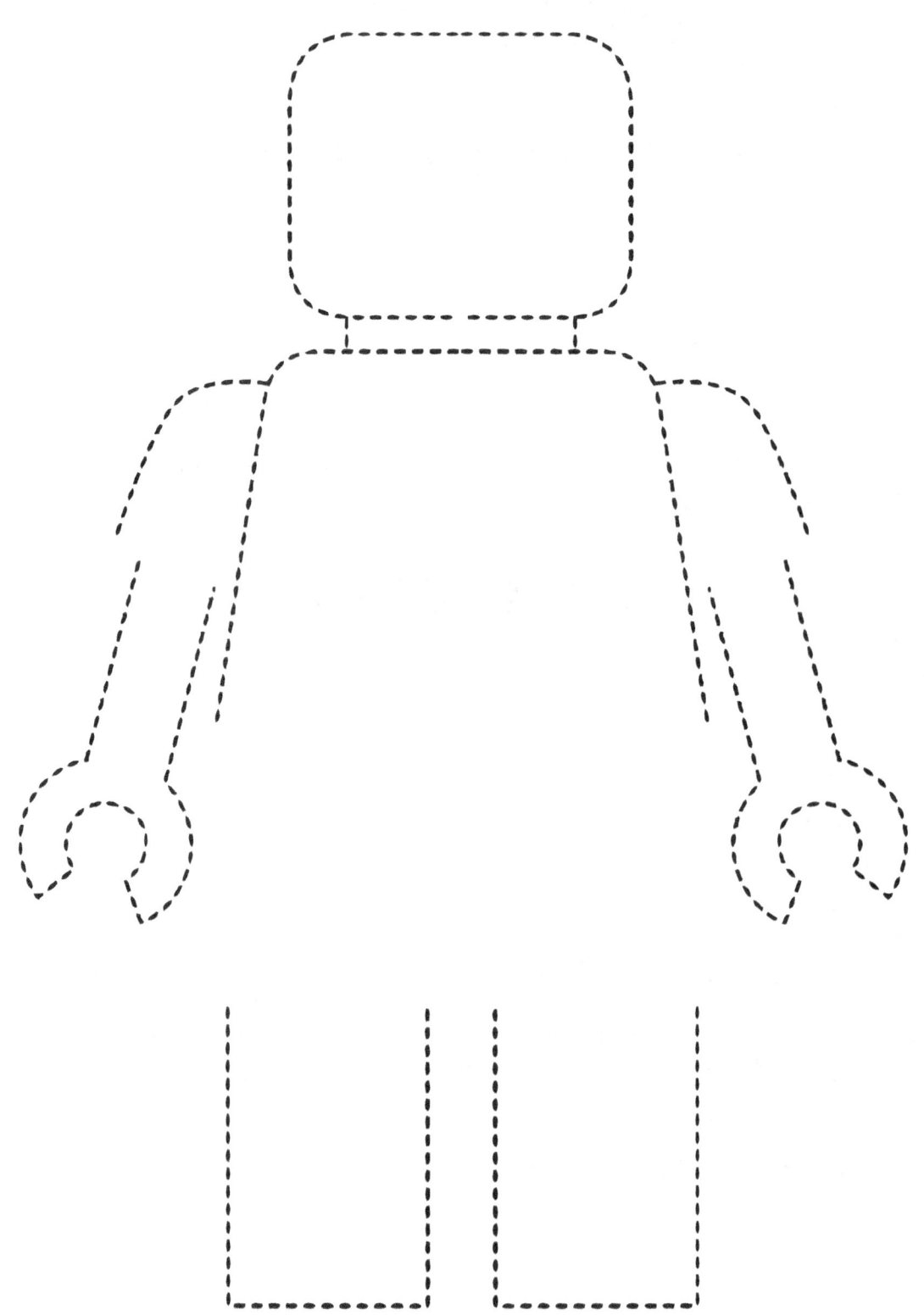

Bazooka Boys ★ Who Am I?

MY TRUE REFLECTION

What's the Point?
I need to see myself the way God sees me.

THEME VERSE:

God, Your thoughts about me are priceless. No one can possibly add them all up.
Psalm 139:17 (NIRV)

RELATED BIBLE PASSAGE:

I Corinthians 13:12

Have you ever noticed that girls look in the mirror **WAY** more than boys? They always seem to be brushing their hair or looking at their clothes. What's up with that? Although some boys are really into their hair and stuff, most of us just look in the mirror when our moms tell us "Go wash your face!"

The mirror can be a good friend. One time I forgot to look in the mirror before I left the house in the morning, and later on in the day I realized that I had two different shoes on! Mirrors can save you from having something in your teeth, something in your hair, and even something in your nose!

> **Good Friend Tip:** Have you ever had a friend with something in his teeth and you weren't sure if you should tell him or not? The answer is this: Friends tell friends! Wouldn't you want to know if YOU had something in YOUR teeth so you could fix it? Find a quiet and non-embarrassing way to point out to your friend what he needs to fix—maybe even lean over and whisper in his ear.

Mirrors are important. They show us what we look like. They show us what we need to fix. They're helpful when we're trying to look our best.

But not all mirrors are helpful.

Have you ever been to a fun house or a fair with a crazy mirror? The ones that make you look super tall or super skinny? Some of them make your head look really big and your legs look really short. Those mirrors are not giving you a true reflection of what you look like. (I sure **HOPE** I don't look like that!) The image you see looking back at you is misshapen and twisted.

And you know what? Sometimes you and I can start looking at ourselves in a "crazy mirror." How we view ourselves can become misshaped and twisted. We can start to think things about ourselves that aren't true at all! When we look in

Bazooka Boys ★ Who Am I?

the mirror, we see someone who isn't strong or talented or smart or funny, but the truth is that isn't who you are at all! The refection you're seeing isn't real. It's CRAZY!

The Bible talks about seeing a reflection that isn't right. I Corinthians 13:12 says, *"Now we see things imperfectly as in a cloudy mirror, but then we will see everything with perfect clarity."* This verse tells us that there are things we think are true (about ourselves and even about God) that aren't accurate. They're a poor reflection that doesn't give us a clear picture.

Today we're going to talk about how important it is that you know your TRUE reflection, that you're looking in an accurate mirror, that you stop looking in a crazy mirror and look to God for a perfect reflection of who you are instead.

Let me ask you a question: What do you think about yourself? Do you think you're strong? Do you think you're good at stuff? Do you think you're smart? What kinds of things do you say about yourself? Do you put yourself down a lot? Are you happy with who you are? Do you compare yourself to other boys and think that you're not as good everyone else?

Sometimes we can be pretty hard on ourselves. We can fill our minds with all the things we're **NOT** and lose site of who we **ARE**. We focus on all the negative things, and pretty soon we don't really see ourselves the way we truly are. We see a distorted, crazy version of ourselves that isn't who we are at all!

Some of you have a really crazy view of yourself. You think a lot of things about yourself that aren't true at all. For whatever reason, you picked up some things along the way and put them on and now the reflection you're seeing in the mirror isn't really you. It's not your true reflection.

So, what should you do? How can you get a real picture of who you are?

 ## 1. STOP PICKING ON YOURSELF.

You know who can be the meanest person in the world to you? You. You know who can pick on you more than any other bully or mean kid? You. You know who can make you feel so bad about yourself you want to cry? You.

We can be so mean to ourselves! We tell ourselves that we're dumb or weak. We tell ourselves that we're not good at anything. We can be super critical of the things we do and say. We beat ourselves up because we aren't as good at something as other boys. We think negative things about the way we look, the way we think, and the things we do.

We've got to **STOP** being so mean to ourselves! Imagine if another boy said all the things to you that you say to yourself? Would you still want to be friends with him? No way! Who would want to be around someone who was always putting you down and pointing out all the negative things about you?

You need to be your own best friend! You need to be encouraging and kind to yourself. You may not be perfect, but there's no reason for you to beat

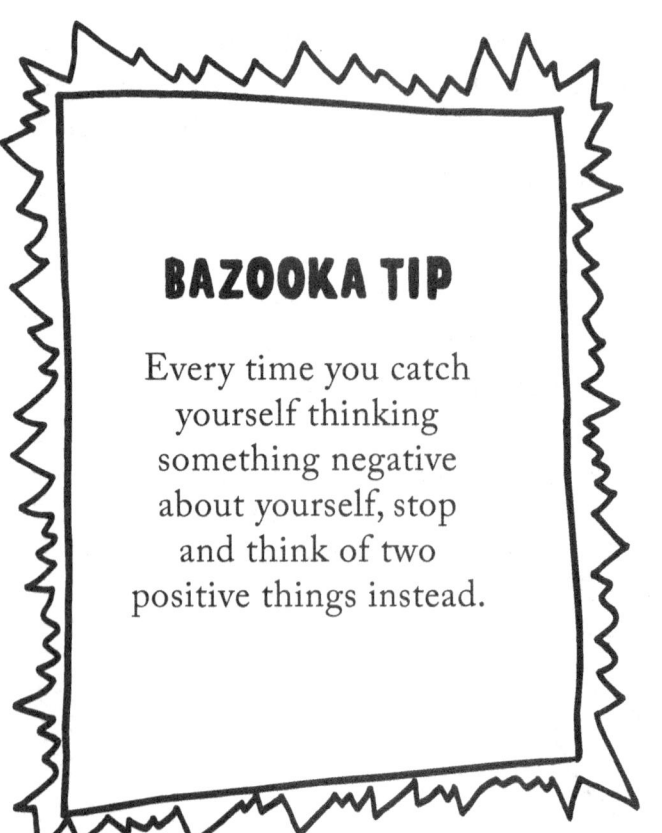

BAZOOKA TIP

Every time you catch yourself thinking something negative about yourself, stop and think of two positive things instead.

yourself up all the time. When you catch yourself thinking something negative, **STOP!** 2 Corinthians 10:5 talks about controlling what we think about. The Bible tells us to take our thoughts captive, which means we need to make sure we're not thinking things that aren't good or healthy for us. And saying negative things about yourself all the time is **NOT** good for you!

Stop focusing on your mistakes and the things you're not good at! Nobody's perfect, and we all have things we're working on. God loves you and doesn't want you picking on His favorite kid—**YOU!**

The best way to see your true reflection is to

 ## 2. KNOW WHAT GOD SAYS ABOUT YOU.

Who knows you the best? Is it your mom? Is it your best friend? Is it your brother? You might think that person knows everything about you, but you know what? God knows you better than **ANYONE!** He knows every thought you have and everything you have ever done or will ever do. God knows you best!

And He thinks you're pretty awesome!

God sees you perfectly. He created you and knows everything about you. His reflection of you is **PERFECT**, so instead of believing that distorted and misshapen image is who you are, why not ask God to give you a **REAL** picture of who you are?

Ask Him to show you **HIS** view of you. Ask Him to remind you how He created you. When other people say things about that aren't true, stop and listen to the voice of God instead. Ask God to show you the way He sees you. Ask Him to help you to hold on to **HIS** image of you and not the crazy picture of yourself you see in your head.

You need to **KNOW** what God says about you! The most important voice in the whole wide world is the voice of God. His view of you is the true reflection of who you are. Everyone else's opinions and comments and even your own view of yourself can be wrong. But God's view of you is perfect.

NO ONE KNOWS YOU LIKE GOD DOES! You need to keep asking Him to show you the way He sees you. When other voices start to play in your head, STOP and listen to the voice of God instead.

You know who HE says you are? He says you're His son. He says you're His friend—a **GOOD** friend. He says you're strong. He says you belong to Him. He says you can do anything because He will help you. He says you're awesome. He says have a purpose. He says you're someone He wants to be around! He says you're His.

Remind yourself how God sees you!

I am God's son *(John 1:12)*

I am a friend of Jesus *(John 15:15)*

I belong to God *(1 Corinthians 6:20)*

I have been chosen by God *(Ephesians 1:3–8)*

I have been forgiven of all my sins *(Colossians 1:13–14)*

I am complete in Christ *(Colossians 2:9–10)*

I have direct access to God *(Hebrews 4:14–16)*

I am free from condemnation *(Romans 8:1–2)*

I cannot be separated from the love of God *(Romans 8:31–39)*

I don't have to be afraid because God has given me a spirit of power, love, and a sound mind *(2 Timothy 1:7)*

I am the house that God lives in *(1 Corinthians 3:16)*

I am God's masterpiece *(Ephesians 2:10)*

I can do all things thorough Christ who strengthens me *(Philippians 4:13)*

That's pretty cool, right? If the God of the universe thinks all those things about you, why would you believe anything else? See yourself the way He sees you.

Bazooka Boys ★ Who Am I?

Closing Prayer: *"Dear God, Thank You that you see me as valuable. Forgive me for being so hard on myself. Help me to stop thinking bad things about who I am, and instead learn to see myself the way You see me. I love you. Amen."*

DOODLE PAGE

LESSON 2

On this mirror, write out some things you've believed about yourself that aren't true."

On this mirror, write out some things that God says about you.

Missing alphabet. Write down the missing letter to find out the verse!

A B C D E F G I J K L M N O P Q R S T U V W X Y Z _____
A B C D E F G H I J K L M N P Q R S T U V W X Y Z _____
A B C D E F G H I J K L M N O P Q R S T U V X Y Z _____

A B C D E F G H I J K L M N O Q R S T U V W X Y Z _____
A B C D E F G H I J K L M N P Q R S T U V W X Y Z _____
A B C D F G H I J K L M N O P Q R S T U V W X Y Z _____
A B D E F G H I J K L M N O P Q R S T U V W X Y Z _____
A B C D E F G H J K L M N O P Q R S T U V W X Y Z _____
A B C D E F G H I J K L M N P Q R S T U V W X Y Z _____
A B C D E F G H I J K L M N O P Q R S T V W X Y Z _____
A B C D E F G H I J K L M N O P Q R T U V W X Y Z _____

B C D E F G H I J K L M N O P Q R S T U V W X Y Z _____
A B C D E F G H I J K L M N O P Q S T U V W X Y Z _____
A B C D F G H I J K L M N O P Q R S T U V W X Y Z _____

A B C D E F G H I J K L M N O P Q R S T U V W X Z _____
A B C D E F G H I J K L M N P Q R S T U V W X Y Z _____
A B C D E F G H I J K L M N O P Q R S T U V W X Y Z _____
A B C D E F G H I J K L M N O P Q S T U V W X Y Z _____

25

A B C D E F G H I J K L M N O P Q R S U V W X Y Z _____
A B C D E F G I J K L M N O P Q R S T U V W X Y Z _____
A B C D E F G H I J K L M N P Q R S T U V W X Y Z _____
A B C D E F G H I J K L M N O P Q R S T V W X Y Z _____
A B C D E F H I J K L M N O P Q R S T U V W X Y Z _____
A B C D E F G I J K L M N O P Q R S T U V W X Y Z _____
A B C D E F G H I J K L M N O P Q R S U V W X Y Z _____
A B C D E F G H I J K L M N O P Q R T U V W X Y Z _____

B C D E F G H I J K L M N O P Q R S T U V W X Y Z _____
A C D E F G H I J K L M N O P Q R S T U V W X Y Z _____
A B C D E F G H I J K L M N P Q R S T U V W X Y Z _____
A B C D E F G H I J K L M N O P Q R S T V W X Y Z _____
A B C D E F G H I J K L M N O P Q R S U V W X Y Z _____

A B C D E F G H I J K L N O P Q R S T U V W X Y Z _____
A B C D F G H I J K L M N O P Q R S T U V W X Y Z _____

A B C D E F G H I J K L M N P Q R S T U V W X Y Z _____

A B C D E F H I J K L M N O P Q R S T U V W X Y Z _____
A B C D E F G H I J K L M N P Q R S T U V W X Y Z _____
A B C E F G H I J K L M N O P Q R S T U V W X Y Z _____

Bazooka Boys ★ Who Am I?

There's a word hidden in each line of letters below. Find each word and write it on the lines to figure out the verse. Once you discover the verse, find it in the Bible and read the entire chapter.

A B B C W H O W D O Y L T S M G V O X Y Z A I
M D O P R E C I O U S G M S U G I M E S T U V J
W U N D A R E S G L T A E F B E R M L M N O J
A P Z A P L A R O A N Y O B Y O U R K G E O R
U V D S P T H O U G H T S J K L M D D T Q E F
X Z Y M E G P R I Y M N A B O U T F O I J K Z I
K E E G H I J P M E C D E F Q R V N P P H L M I
Y B B C Q L O W D G Y L T S M G V J X Y Z H B
R L A C J F P T S M U G O G O D A E I O U B K E
P R B A J G H P S A L M Q R T Z Y J K C F H I K

___ ___ ___   ___ ___ ___ ___ ___ ___ ___   ___ ___ ___
    Line 1   Line 2   Line 3

___ ___ ___   ___ ___ ___ ___ ___ ___ ___ ___
    Line 4   Line 5

___ ___ ___ ___ ___   ___ ___   ___   ___ ___ ___ .
    Line 6   Line 7   Line 8   Line 9

___ ___ ___ ___ ___ 139:17
    Line 10

Go to the Bible and read each Scripture reference to find the answers to the crossword clues.

Bazooka Boys ★ Who Am I?

WEEK 2

Down

1. *I can do all things through Christ who _____ me (Philippians 4:13)*

2. *I _____ to God (1 Corinthians 6:20)*

3. *I am the _____ that God lives in (1 Corinthians 3:16)*

4. *I am _____ in Christ (Colossians 2:9-10)*

5. *I have direct _____ to God (Hebrews 4:14-16)*

6. *I am a _____ of Jesus (John 15:15)*

8. *I am God's _____ (John 1:12)*

12. *I don't have to be afraid because God has given me a _____ of power, love, and sound mind. (2 Timothy 1:7)*

Across

6. *I am _____ from condemnation (Romans 8:1-2)*

7. *I have been _____ of all my sins (Colossians 1:13-14)*

9. *I am God's _____ (Ephesians 2:10)*

10. *I cannot be separated from the _____ of God (Romans 8:31-39)*

11. *I have been _____ by God (Ephesians 1:3-8)*

WORD LIST

forgiven *love* *house*
son *friend* *belong*
spirit *chosen* *complete*
access *strengthens*
masterpiece *free*

29

BAZOOKA BREAKDOWN

Have you ever been to a carnival and see those crazy mirrors that make you look super weird? On the fun house mirror below – draw the craziest, funniest, weirdest picture of yourself you can think of.

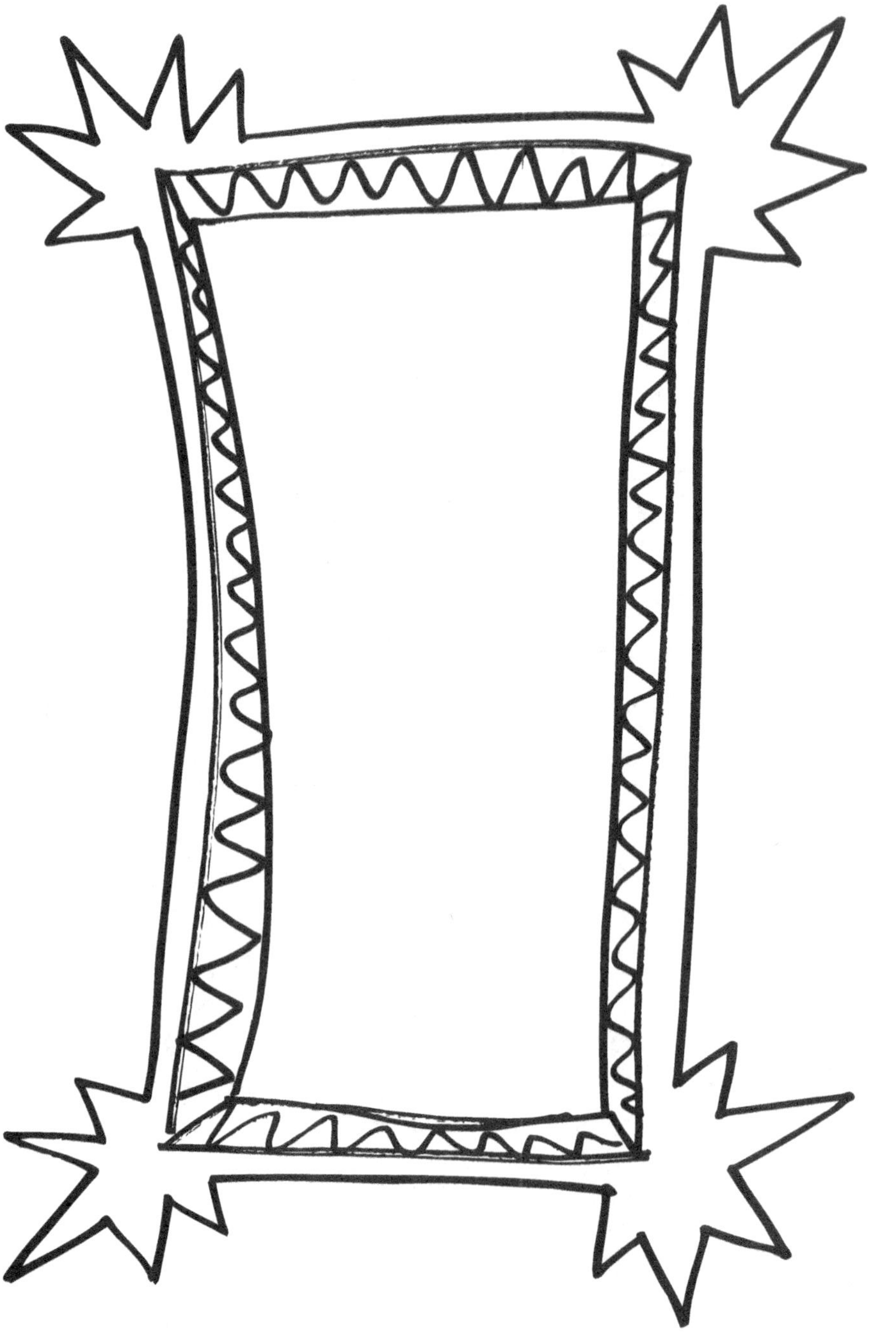

Bazooka Boys ★ Who Am I?

Sometimes we see ourselves in ways that may not necessarily be true. Someone calls you a name and it sticks. People treat you a certain way and it makes you feel like you're a loser. You don't get picked for a team and you decide you're just not good enough. In the bubbles below, list some of the places we get our crazy views of ourselves.

We need to remember the things that God says about us and let go of those negative images we see in the mirror. In the list below, write your name in the blank to remember who God says you are!

_____ is God's son (John 1:12)

_____ is a friend of Jesus (John 15:15)

_____ belongs to God (1 Corinthians 6:20)

_____ has been chosen by God (Ephesians 1:3-8)

_____ has been forgiven of all his sins (Colossians 1:13-14)

_____ is complete in Christ (Colossians 2:9-10)

_____ has direct access to God (Hebrews 4:14-16)

_____ is free from condemnation (Romans 8:1-2)

_____ cannot be separated from the love of God (Romans 8:31-39)

WEEK 2

_____ doesn't have to be afraid, because God has given him a spirit of power, love, and a sound mind (2 Timothy 1:7)

_____ is the house that God lives in (1 Corinthians 3:16)

_____ is God's masterpiece (Ephesians 2:10)

_____ can do all things thorough Christ who strengthens him (Philippians 4:13)

Write out the verse below three times and see if you can memorize it!
"God, your thoughts about me are priceless. No one can possibly add them all up."
–Psalm 139:17 (NIRV)

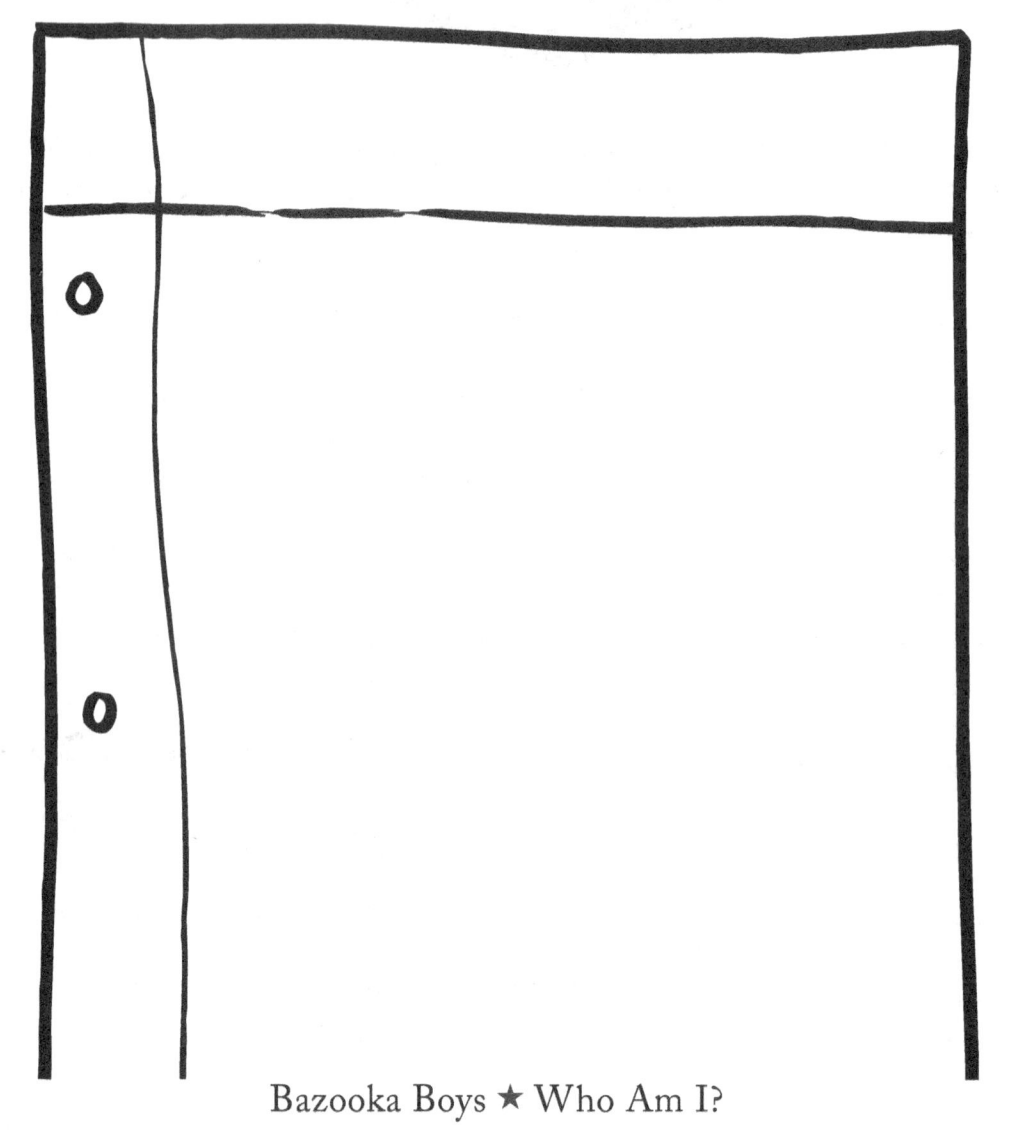

Bazooka Boys ★ Who Am I?

BAZOOKA PROJECT

WEEK 2

OPTION 1: POP THOSE THOUGHTS

Supplies

- Balloons
- Markers
- Pen

Directions

1. Blow up the balloon and secure the end.

2. Write all the negative thoughts that go through your mind about yourself on the balloon.

3. Now, make your balloon pop! Poke it with a pen, jump on it, squeeze it!

4. Remember that God values you and does NOT want you to think negative thoughts about yourself.

OPTION 2: DESTROY THIS JOURNAL!

Supplies

- Template (provided)
- Paper clips
- Crayons/markers
- Stapler

Directions

Color the front of your journal with markers/crayons and follow the instructions on each page provided.

Bazooka Boys ★ Who Am I?

DESTROY THIS JOURNAL

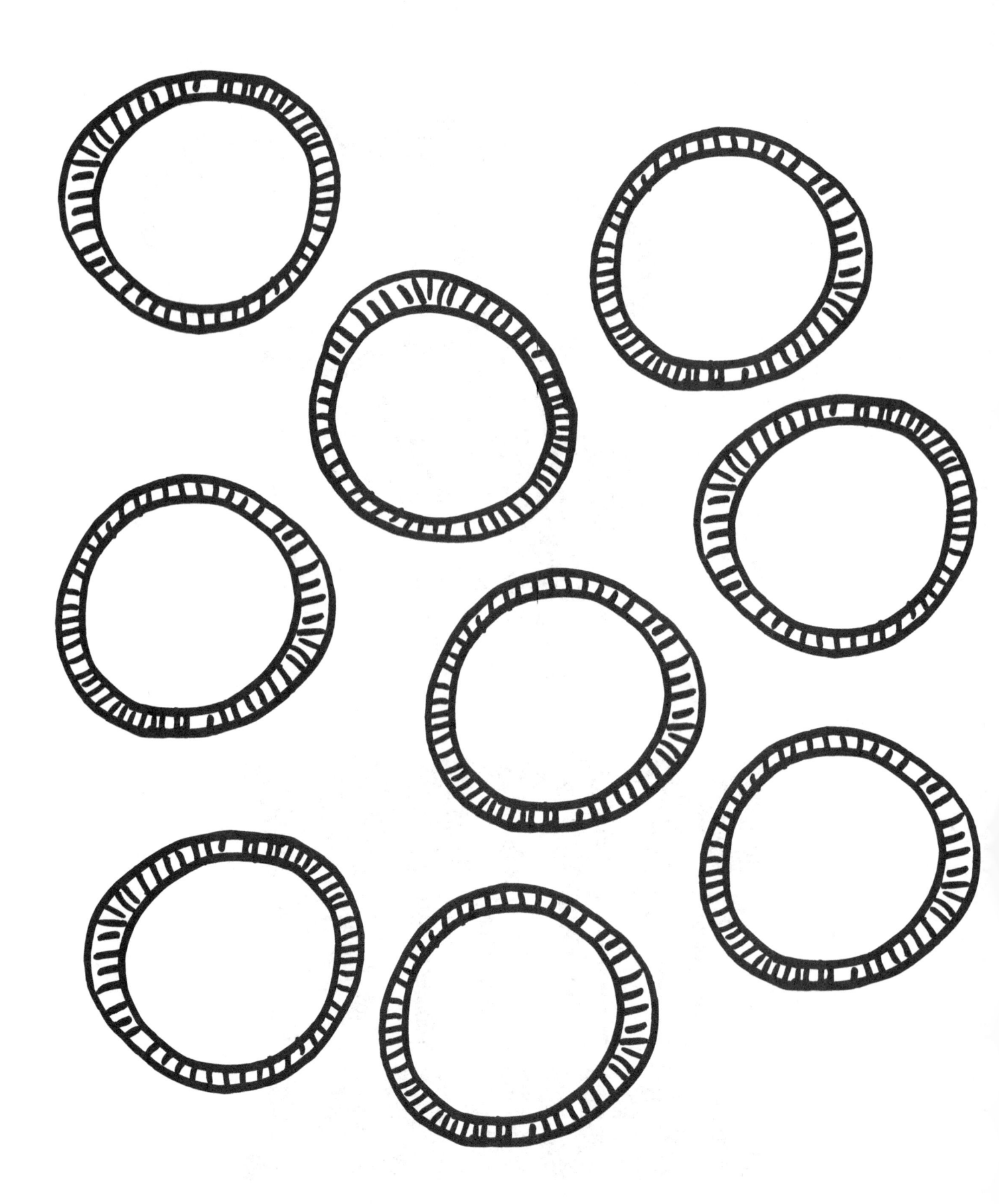

In the circles write down your negative thoughts. **POKE HOLES** in them with your pencil.

Write down the negative things other people say about you and **JUMP**
ON THIS PAGE WITH YOUR DIRTY SHOES.

Write down all the things you think you are not good at and SMEAR YOUR FOOD AND DRINK ALL OVER EACH THING!

WRITE DOWN ALL THE COOL THINGS GOD SAYS ABOUT YOU. Write them over and over in the coolest colors and designs.

WHO AM I?

WEEK 3

WHATEVER!

WHAT'S THE POINT?
YOU DON'T HAVE TO BELIEVE THE THINGS OTHER PEOPLE SAY ABOUT YOU.

THEME VERSE:
If God is for us, who can ever be against us?
Romans 8:31

RELATED BIBLE PASSAGE:
Daniel 6

Joshua didn't know what to think. He had moved to a new school over the summer and now found himself in a totally new place where everything was different. At his old school, he knew everyone and had lots of friends. Things couldn't be more different now.

For some reason, a couple of the boys decided they did **NOt** like him. They refused to let him sit at their table at lunch. They picked on him during recess. Worst of all, they started saying things about him that weren't true.

They said he cheated on his homework. They said he was a wimp. And then they started saying bad things about his family.

Joshua was so upset! How could people he barely knew have it in for him? Why would someone say such horrible things about him? He had never, ever cheated before! He didn't think he was better than everyone—he was a good friend! And the things that were said about his family were just plain old lies.

The hardest part about all of it was that Joshua started to believe the rumors himself. At first he was angry, but as time went on, he was just hurt and the more hurt he got, the more he started to think that maybe those people were right about him. Maybe he was a wimp. Maybe he wasn't a very good friend. Maybe his family wasn't the greatest. In his heart he knew those things weren't

Bazooka Boys ★ Who Am I?

true, but sometimes when you hear things enough, you start to wonder if maybe they are true.

Have you ever had anyone say something not-so-nice about you?

It can be really easy to believe what other people say about you. You can have all kinds of unkind things said about you—about how smart you are or how cool you are (or aren't), whether or not you're good at something, and even if you're a good friend.

I don't know why people can be so mean to each other. I wish it didn't happen. But the truth is, sometimes people are just mean. They say things that hurt our feelings and make us feel bad about ourselves.

There are **LOTS** of stories in the Bible of people who had to overcome what other people said about them. There was Joseph, who was accused of doing things he had never done. There was David, whose brothers didn't want him around at all. There was Daniel, who was hated so much by other people that they created a trap so he would be thrown into a den of lions!

These men had to let God help them work through these things. God helped Joseph be smart and run from the woman who was trying to trap him. God helped David defeat Goliath right in front of his brothers. God shut the mouths of the lions and saved Daniel's life!

God will help you work through it too. In the times when you face people being mean and saying things that make you feel bad, the Holy Spirit will make you strong. He'll help you know what to do in those situations.

So, what do you do when someone says something about you that hurts your feelings or makes you feel bad about yourself?

> **PLACE ME LIKE A SEAL OVER YOUR HEART.**
> **SONG OF SOLOMON 8:6**

The first thing you need to do is

1. LET GO OF THE HURTFUL THINGS PEOPLE SAY ABOUT YOU.

When someone says something about you that hurts your feelings or makes you feel like you're not good at something, it's easy to keep thinking about it over and over again. You can replay those words or actions in your mind and continue to feel bad about it.

Instead of holding onto those unkind words, why don't you try just letting them go? Every time you start to think about it, stop yourself and say, "No way! I'm not going to think about that anymore!"

Have you ever gotten a balloon that has helium in it? What happens if you let it go? It flies up to the sky, right? What if, when someone says or does something to you that hurts your feelings, you imagine that you put all those unkind words or actions into a balloon and let it go up into the sky and fly right up to Jesus? Instead of holding on to them and replaying them in your mind, just let them go instead. Send up all those hurtful things and let Jesus take them out of your heart and mind. I promise it will help you feel better!

Jesus is the **VERY** best at helping you through something that has hurt you. If you keep bringing those thing things to Him, He will help you feel better.

A while ago, I hurt my finger. I had a really big cut on my hand and man-oh-man did it hurt. The only thing that would make it feel better is if I took a Band-Aid and wrapped it really, really tight around the cut. If I took the Band-Aid off, it would start to hurt again. So I would put on another really tight bandage to help it feel better.

There is a verse in the Bible that says that God will be like a big Band-Aid to your heart when your feelings are hurt. Song of Solomon 8:6 says, *"Place me like a seal over your heart."* When you're feeling bad about something someone has said or done to you, run to Jesus and let Him wrap Himself around your heart like a big Band-Aid. He will help your heart get better and He will help it not hurt as much, too. He loves you and wants to help you work through the hard stuff you go through sometimes.

So, let go of the things that people say, and let Jesus help your heart feel better.

The second thing you need to do when someone says or does something that hurts your feeling is

2. FORGIVE THE PEOPLE WHO HURT YOU.

Some of you have had really hurtful things said to you. You have been teased. Someone has picked on you and embarrassed you in front of other people. It can be so hard to understand why people would hurt you and make you feel bad. Sometimes it just doesn't make sense and the **LAST** thing you want to do is forgive someone who has made you feel so horrible.

But the Bible says we're supposed to **FORGIVE** the people who hurt us. Colossians 3:13 says, *"Make allowance for each other's faults, and forgive anyone who offends you. Remember, the Lord forgave you, so you must forgive others."*

This is **NOT** an easy thing to do, is it? We don't want to forgive them—we want to get back at them! We want them to feel bad for hurting us. But the Bible says we're supposed forgive them! We're supposed to let go of the desire to get back and get even and trust that God will take care of us. Proverbs 20:22 says, *"Don't say, 'I will get even for this wrong.' Wait for the LORD to handle the matter."*

As much as you want to hold onto your anger and hurt, and as much as you want to see the person who has hurt you feel bad, Jesus says you have to forgive them. To forgive someone means to stop being mad at them and to not hope something bad will happen to them. On our own, it is really, really hard to forgive someone, but Jesus will help you forgive the people who have hurt you.

The last thing you should do when someone says or does something to you that hurts you is

3. LEARN tO SAY "YOU'RE NOt MY MUDDER!"

You're probably wondering, "What in the world does that mean?" I'll tell you!

When my daughter Betty was about four years old, she loved to boss her older brother Charlie around. Charlie was seven, and his little sister definitely knew how to get him upset.

Her favorite thing to do was to tell him that he had to turn off his video games. She would march up in front of the television set and say, "Charlie! You have to turn off your games **RIGHT NOW** or you are going to be grounded." She would put her hand on her hip and shake her finger in his face and make sure he knew she was **NOt** happy with him.

Charlie would come running to me so upset saying, "Betty says that I have to turn off my video games! I just got started!" I would assure him that he **DIDN't** have to turn off his games yet, but he would just look at me so sad and say, "But Betty says I have to."

Finally, I had enough. I said to Charlie, "Betty is **NOT** your mother. I am your mother. Just because she **ACTS** like she's the boss of you and **THINKS** she's the boss of you **DOESN't** make her the boss of you. She's not your mother and you don't have to do what she says." He seemed to understand what I was saying to him and a little while later, I heard Betty trying to boss him around again. Charlie looked her right in the eye and said, "You're not my mudder!"

Bazooka Boys ★ Who Am I?

A few weeks later, I was dealing with someone who had said something about me that hurt my feelings. They said something that wasn't true, and I was starting to believe what they had said. I mean, they sure acted pretty sure of themselves—maybe they were right. Suddenly, I said out loud, "You know what? You're not my mudder!"

> YOU'RE NOT MY MUDDER!

Just because someone says something about you doesn't make it true. Just because someone says that you act a certain way doesn't make it true. Just because someone acts like the boss of you doesn't mean they are.

I've learned that when people say things about me, I have to stop myself and ask, "Is what they're saying about me true?" If it's not, then I say, "You're not my mudder!" I refuse to believe something that isn't true or kind just because someone else says it. Instead of believing the lie or sitting quietly by and letting them talk about you, don't be afraid to look them right in the eye and say, "Whatever! You don't know what you're talking about." It's okay to stand up for yourself!

Learn to say to yourself, "**I KNOW** who I am and I refuse to believe what they're saying about me." You have to **KNOW** who you are, not who other people **SAY** you are, not who other people **THINK** you are, not who other people **WANT** you to be. Know **WHO YOU ARE**.

WHO are you? You are **AWESOME!** You have something to offer the world. You are worth knowing. God made you for a purpose, and He has plans for your life. God is for you. He believes in you and thinks you're **AMAZING**. Romans 8:31 says, "*If God is for us, who can ever be against us?*" It doesn't matter what anyone else says about you because you know God knows you best and loves you most.

Some of you have been really hurt by the things other people have said or done to you. God wants to help you let go of those things and let Him heal the hurt in your heart. He wants to help you forgive the people who have said or done mean things to you.

Some of you have allowed yourselves to believe what other people have said about you. You're feeling bad about what you look like or what your abilities are or even what your family is like because of the things people have said. Today, Jesus wants to give you the strength and courage to say "You're not my mudder!" to the people who are trying to hurt you and instead stand confidently in who God created you to be. He wants you to stand proudly as the cool kid who He made you to be.

Closing Prayer: *"Dear God, I've been hurt by the things other people have said about me. Help me to let go of those things and not believe the lies. Please heal my heart and help me forgive the people who have hurt me. Give me the strength to stand up and not believe the lies that are said about me. I love You. Amen."*

DOODLE PAGE

LESSON 3

On the rocket ship, write out some of the things people have said or done that have hurt you. If you don't want to write them out, draw a symbol that will help you imagine what those things are. Then imagine that rocket ship flying up to Jesus! Color in the rocket and the theme verse.

IF GOD IS FOR US WHO CAN EVER BE AGAINST US?

— ROMANS 8:31

Bazooka Boys ★ Who Am I?

ACTIVITY SHEET

WEEK 3

Search the Chart

	A	B	C	D	E	F
1	If	the	spirit	and	can	care
2	to	against	now	above	you	don't
3	have	people	don't	ever	God	believe
4	about	say	things	can	Romans	forgive
5	right	is	Jesus	name	know	us
6	trust	for	so	who	be	?

Find the words on the chart and write them below to discover the verse. Check your answer by reading Romans 8:31.

_____	_____	_____	_____	_____
A/1	E/3	B/5	B/6	F/5

_____	_____	_____	_____	_____
D/6	E/1	D/3	E/6	B/2

_____	_____	_____	8:31
F/5	F/6	E/4	

"Whatever" Scriptures

Look up the verses below and fill in the missing words:

If God is for us, who can ever be _____ us? —Romans 8:31

Finally, brothers and sisters, whatever is _____, whatever is noble, whatever is right, whatever is pure, whatever is lovely, whatever is admirable—if anything is excellent or praiseworthy—_____ about such things.
—Philippians 4:8 NIV

Place me like a _____ over your heart... —Solomon 8:6

Don't say, "I will get _____ for this wrong. Wait for the LORD to handle the matter. —Proverbs 20:22

Make allowance for each other's faults, and _____ anyone who offends you. Remember, the Lord forgave you, so you must forgive others.
—Colossians 3:13

For I know the plans I have for you," says the LORD. "They are plans for _____ and not for disaster, to give you a future and a hope.
—Jeremiah 29:11

Obviously, I'm not trying to win the _____ of people, but of God. If pleasing people were my goal, I would not be Christ's servant. —Galatians 1:10

BAZOOKA BREAKDOWN

WEEK 3

Have you ever had sometime say or do something mean to you? How did you feel when that happened? Circle the words that describe your reaction.

- SAD
- CONFUSED
- REVENGEFUL
- MAD
- FRUSTRATED
- SCARED
- EMBARRASSED
- HURT

What does it mean to forgive someone? Write out your thoughts below.

Write out this verse three times and see if you can memorize it!

"If God is for us, who can ever be against us?"
—Romans 8:31

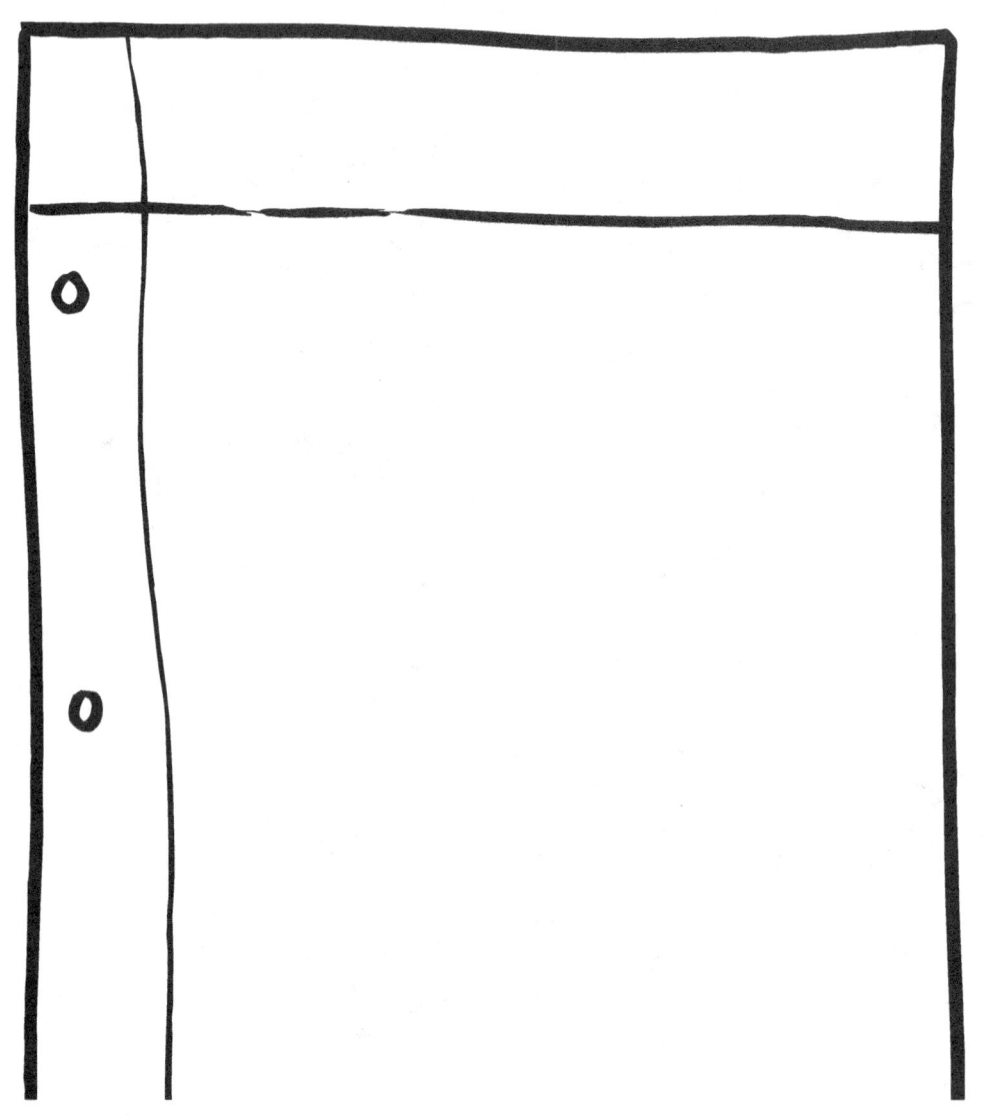

Bazooka Boys ★ Who Am I?

BAZOOKA PROJECT

OPTION 1: WHATEVER! MINI MARSHMALLOW SHOOTER

Supplies

- 9 oz plastic cups or yogurt containers
- 12" balloons
- Mini marshmallows
- Scissors

Directions

1. Cut the bottom off the plastic cup or container. (If using plastic cups, it works best if the cups are doubled up.)

2. Cut off the bottom third of the cup or yogurt container and discard top portion.

3. Tie a knot at the end of each balloon and cut off about 1/2" from the top of the balloon.

4. Stretch the balloon over the top end of the cup or container. The balloon knot will be on the top.

5. Holding the bottom of the cup towards the sky, place the mini marshmallows in the cup.

6. Pull back on the knot and launch the marshmallows!

OPTION 2: WHATEVER! STOMP ART

Supplies
- Tempera paint
- Easel paper
- Tape
- Scissors
- Paintbrush
- Paper plate
- Bubble wrap

Directions

1. To set up the painting surface, roll out two or three long lengths of easel paper next to each other.

2. Squirt one or two colors of paint onto a paper plate.

3. Cut a length of bubble wrap, wide enough to make a little boot for your foot.

4. Loosely wrap and tape the bubble wrap around each boy's foot. (you might find it easier to only do one foot and keep the other clean)

5. Using the paintbrush, paint the bubble wrap on the bottom of your foot.

6. Now it's time to paint! Walk, stomp, jump across the paper with your bubble wrapped feet.

WHO AM I?

WEEK 4

EVERY-BODY

What's the Point?
God made your body and you should take care of it.

THEME VERSE

Dear friends, God is good. So I beg you to offer your bodies to him as a living sacrifice, pure and pleasing. That's the most sensible way to serve God. Don't be like the people of this world, but let God change the way you think. Then you will know how to do everything that is good and pleasing to Him.
—Romans 12:1–2 (CEV)

RELATED BIBLE STORY

1 Corinthians 1:18–31

If you could change one thing about the way you look, what would it be? Maybe you think you're too tall or too skinny. Maybe you think you're too short or your hair is too curly. Maybe you think your nose is too big or your ears are too small. Maybe you think your skin is the wrong color or your feet are the wrong size.

Most of us have SOMETHING we don't like about our bodies. There are things about us that make us feel different. We don't look like the boys on TV or the popular kids at school. It's really easy to point out all the things about our physical appearance that we just wish were different!

There's a verse in the Bible that says this exact thing! Romans 9:20 says, "*Should what is formed say to Him who formed it, 'Why did You make me like this?'*" Have you ever asked God that question—"Why did You make me like this?" I sure have.

In this chapter, we're going to look at the way we view our appearance and how we can have a healthy perspective of our bodies and the unique way God made each and every one of us.

So, what is your body image? Basically, it's the way you see and feel about the way you look. It's how you view yourself. We get our body image from the things other people say to us, from the things we see in magazines and on TV, and the way we think we measure up to those images.

Bazooka Boys ★ Who Am I?

WEEK 4

Maybe you've seen a picture of someone you think is really athletic and now you struggle with feeling bad because you don't look the same as that picture. Maybe at school, everyone likes the boys who look a certain way, and because you don't look like that, you don't like yourself very much. Your body image—the way you see yourself—is shaped by what other people think (or by what you **THINK** other people **THINK!**).

But God wants you to have a **GOOD** body image. He made you unique, and He doesn't want you feeling bad about the way you look!

So, how can you overcome a negative body image? How can you feel better about the way you look? What can you do to accept and love the body God gave you? We're going to look at a verse in the Bible that tells us three things that can help us be okay with the way we look.

"Dear friends, God is good. So I beg you to offer your bodies to him as a living sacrifice, pure and pleasing. That's the most sensible way to serve God. Don't be like the people of this world, but let God change the way you think. Then you will know how to do everything that is good and pleasing to Him."—Romans 12:1–2 (CEV)

The first thing you need to do to have a healthy body image is to

1. CHANGE THE WAY YOU THINK.

Have you ever learned something one way, and then had to learn a different way to do the same thing? My kids brought home some math homework and when I sat down to help them, it didn't take me long to realize that the teachers had taught them a different way to solve the problems than the way I learned when I was in school. Every time I look at a problem, I automatically start thinking about it in a certain way, and then I have to stop and make myself think about the **NEW** way to answer the question. It's not easy because my mind tends to think a certain way (and my kids like to tease me about it, too!).

If you have a certain way of thinking about things, it can be hard to stop thinking that way and change your thoughts. But that's EXACTLY what you need to do when it comes to your body image. You need to change how you think about the way you look. It can be so easy to think the worst about yourself. You can constantly put yourself down and look for the negative things about your body and appearance.

Instead of always thinking about the negative, what if you thought about the things you like? Instead of comparing yourself to other boys, what if you decided that it's okay to be you? The Bible says God will help us feel peaceful about the way we look if we **FIX** our thoughts on Him and who He created us to be. Isaiah 26:3 says, *"You will keep in perfect peace all who trust in You, all whose thoughts are fixed on You."*

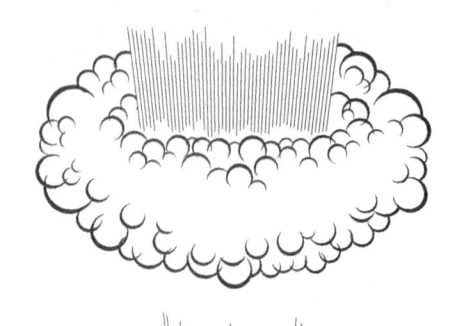

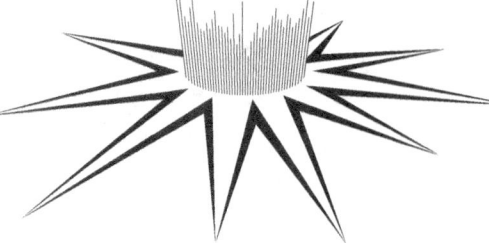

When you start to think something negative about yourself, STOP yourself and then change your thoughts to something positive! When you begin to compare yourself to the boys on TV, fix your mind on the fact that God created you just the way He wanted you to be. Ask God to help you to change the way you think about your body and appearance. He will help you!

The second way we can have a healthy body image is

2. DON'T BE LIKE THE PEOPLE OF THE WORLD.

Answer this for me: Who decides what's cool? Who decides what's popular? Who decides who's good looking and who's not good looking? It's kind of a silly question, isn't it? I don't really know the answer. I guess a lot of times we decide what's cool and good looking based on what we see on TV or magazines. But **WHY?** Why do the people who make the TV shows and magazines get to decide what's cool? Who are these people and why do they get to decide whether or not I'm cool? It's pretty silly if you ask me.

The Bible says we're to "not be like the people of the world." This means that we're not supposed to strive to be what the world tells us is popular or cool. 1 Corinthians 1:28 tells us, *"What the world thinks is worthless, useless, and nothing at all is what God has used to destroy what the world considers important."* (CEV) Instead of focusing on what the world says is cool, we should focus on what God says is cool!

What does God say is cool? Well, let's take a look around. God created us all so different, didn't He? If He wanted us to all look the same, He would have created us that way! But He didn't. He made us unique and a million different shades of awesome.

> "YOU WILL KEEP IN PERFECT PEACE ALL WHO TRUST IN YOU, ALL WHOSE THOUGHTS ARE FIXED ON YOU."
> —ISAIAH 26:3

I want you to think about how many different sports there are in the world. Now, I have a question for you. Which sport is the best?

The answer is this: All of them. Each one is different, but cool and exciting in its own way. They're not the same, but they are fun. Even though they're all different from each other, each one teaches us something different. You may have a personal favorite, but that doesn't mean that the other sports aren't just as cool!

You and I thinking we have to look a certain way to be cool is just like us saying that the **ONLY** sport that's awesome is football. Yes, football ROCKS, but it isn't the **ONLY** cool sport!

You may look different than your friends. You may look different than the boys on TV. But who says that means you aren't cool? That's just silly.

We need to stop looking to the world to tell us what's cool. God has SHOWED us what's cool through the way He created us—unique and different. Let's stop thinking that we have to look like what the world says and embrace God's view of creative awesomeness!

So, you should change the way you think, stop believing what the world says about what's cool, and you should

3. OFFER YOUR BODY TO GOD AS A LIVING SACRIFICE

I bet you're wondering what a sacrifice is. In the Old Testament, people used to come to the Temple to bring a gift for God—that gift was called a sacrifice or an offering. Now, they didn't just bring any old offering, they would select the very best animal or food they had and give it to God to show Him that they loved Him. It was something they had taken good care of and gave willingly to God out of their devotion to Him.

So, what does it mean to offer your **BODY** as a living sacrifice to God? It means that you need to tell God that your body belongs to Him. Take good care of it because you want to give Him the very best you have to offer. Give God your body so you can do anything He may ask of you.

Bazooka Boys ★ Who Am I?

You see, God has a **HUGE, GINORMOUS** plan for your life. He has given you gifts and talents that are all housed inside the physical body He has given you. He wants you to use the things He has given you to accomplish all kinds of amazing things!

If you're not taking care of your body, then you can't give God your very best sacrifice. If you're putting it down all the time and hating things about your offering, then you're not bringing a very good sacrifice to God. If you're not honoring the body God gave you by making sure you're not doing anything that can harm you, you're not bringing a very good sacrifice to God.

I don't know about you, but I want to give God the very best I have. I want to give Him a body I'm proud of. I want to give Him a body that's ready to do anything He may ask of me! I want to give Him the very best sacrifice I can.

Instead of being negative and critical about the way you look, choose to think positive things about the way God made you! Refuse to buy into the world's way of thinking that says we all have to look alike. Take good care of the body God has given you so you can do great things for Him!

Closing Prayer: "Dear God, I thank You for the body You gave me. I know You made me special and unique. Help me to change the way I think about the way I look. I want to see things the way **YOU** see them, not the way the world sees them. I offer my body as a sacrifice for You because I love You. Amen."

DOODLE PAGE

LESSON 4

All superheroes have a super hideout! It's the place where they live and keep all their super cool super hero stuff. The Bible says your body is "the Temple of the Holy Spirit" (1 Corinthians 6:19). A temple is basically the house where God lives—it's **HIS** super hideout! God lives in your body, so your body is God's house! In the space below, draw a house that shows what your super hideout would look like. Create cool gadgets and gizmos that show what's unique about you! Remember—God lives inside of **YOU**!

ACTIVITY SHEET

WEEK 4

The pictures below are symbols of words that will help you understand how God wants you to view your body.

Ask your mom or dad to help you figure out the missing words by cutting out the symbol *(on page 67)* and placing it in the correct sentence to complete the special message from God.

Dear
[ ]
,
God is good.

So I beg you to offer your
[ ]
to Him as a living sacrifice, pure and pleasing.

That's the most sensible way to
[ ]
God.

Don't be like the people of this
[ ]
,
but let God change the way you think.

Bazooka Boys ★ Who Am I?

WEEK 4

"Dear Friends, God is good. So I beg you to offer your bodies to Him as a living sacrifice, pure and pleasing, the most sensible way to serve God. Don't be like the people of this world, but let God change the way you think. Then you will know how to do everything that is good and pleasing to Him."
—Romans 12:1–2 (CEV)

Bazooka Boys ★ Who Am I?

WEEK 4

Unscramble the words and sentences below to reveal God's Word. Try not to look!

Step 1: Unscramble the words.

ccrasiife	gslpaine	efsidrn	sreve
_____	_____	_____	_____

dbiseo	ynveheirtg	gdoo	rfofe
_____	_____	_____	_____

lppeeo	gehnca
_____	_____

Dear _____, God is good. So I beg you to _____ your _____ to Him as a living _____, pure and _____. That's the most sensible way to _____ God. Don't be like the _____ of this world, but let God _____ the way you think. Then you will know how to do _____ that is _____ and _____ to Him. —Romans 12:1–2 (CEV)

Step 2: Put the unscrambled words into the correct sentence below.

Don't be like the _____ of this world, but let God _____ the way you think.

So I beg you to _____ your _____ to Him as a living _____, pure and _____.

Dear _____, God is good.

Then you will know how to do _____ that is _____ and _____ to Him.

That's the most sensible way to _____ God.

Step 3: Write the sentences in the correct order to reveal God's word to you!

_____
_____
_____
_____
_____
_____
_____
_____
_____
_____

Bazooka Boys ★ Who Am I?

BAZOOKA BREAKDOWN

WEEK 4

What do you look like? In the space below, draw a picture of yourself. Highlight at least 6 things that describe your appearance. Remember to be positive!

The Bible says that we are to offer our bodies to God as a living sacrifice. That means we give our very best. What are some ways you can take **REALLY** good care of your body?

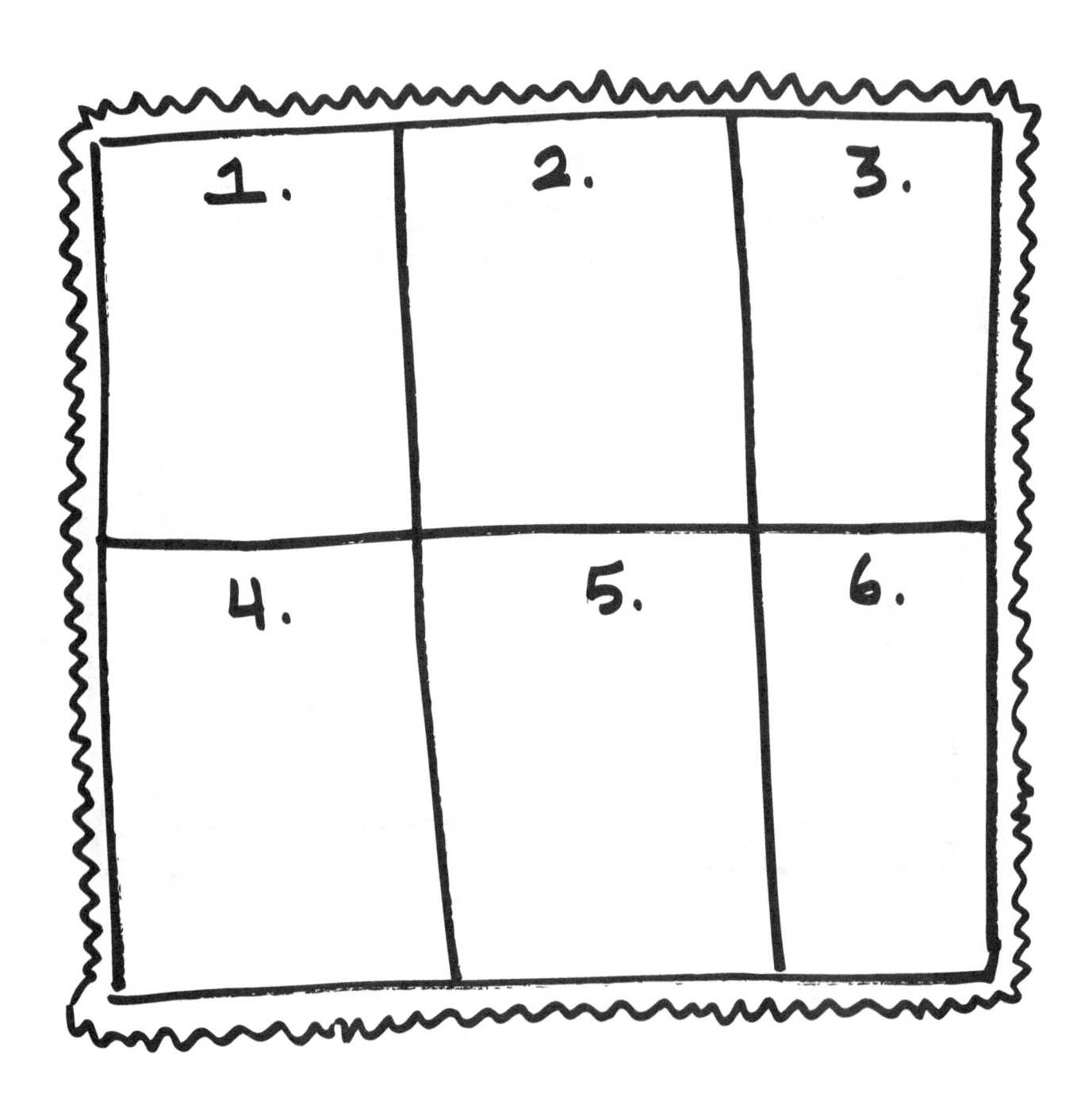

1.	2.	3.
4.	5.	6.

Bazooka Boys ★ Who Am I?

WEEK 4

Write out this verse three times and do your best to memorize it!

"*¹Dear friends, God is good. So I beg you to offer your bodies to him as a living sacrifice, pure and pleasing. That's the most sensible way to serve God. ²Don't be like the people of this world, but let God change the way you think. Then you will know how to do everything that is good and pleasing to him.*"
—Romans 12:1–2

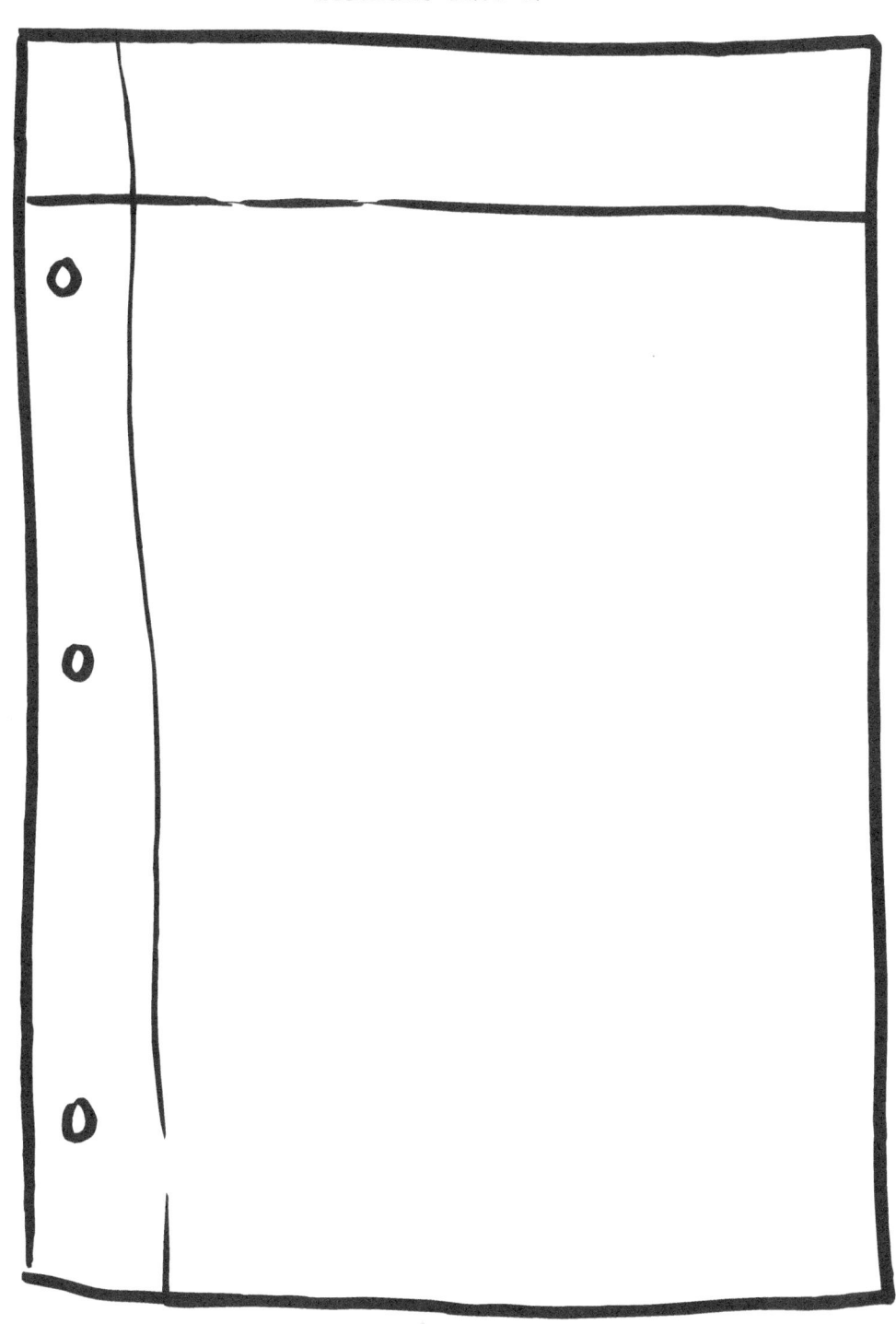

Bazooka Boys ★ Who Am I?

BAZOOKA PROJECT

WEEK 4

EVERY BODY FINGERPRINT ART

Supplies:
- White cardstock
- Different colors of non-toxic ink pads
- Markers/crayons
- Fine point black Sharpies

Directions:

1. Using non-toxic ink, finish the picture with your fingerprints.
   - Football field—create players and/or footballs
   - Baseball field—create players and/or baseballs
   - Zoo—finish the bodies of the animals
   - Cityscape—add the heads to their super heroes bodies
2. Add dimension to the fingerprints by using the sharpie marker to add specific features.
3. Color the rest of the picture using crayons/makers.

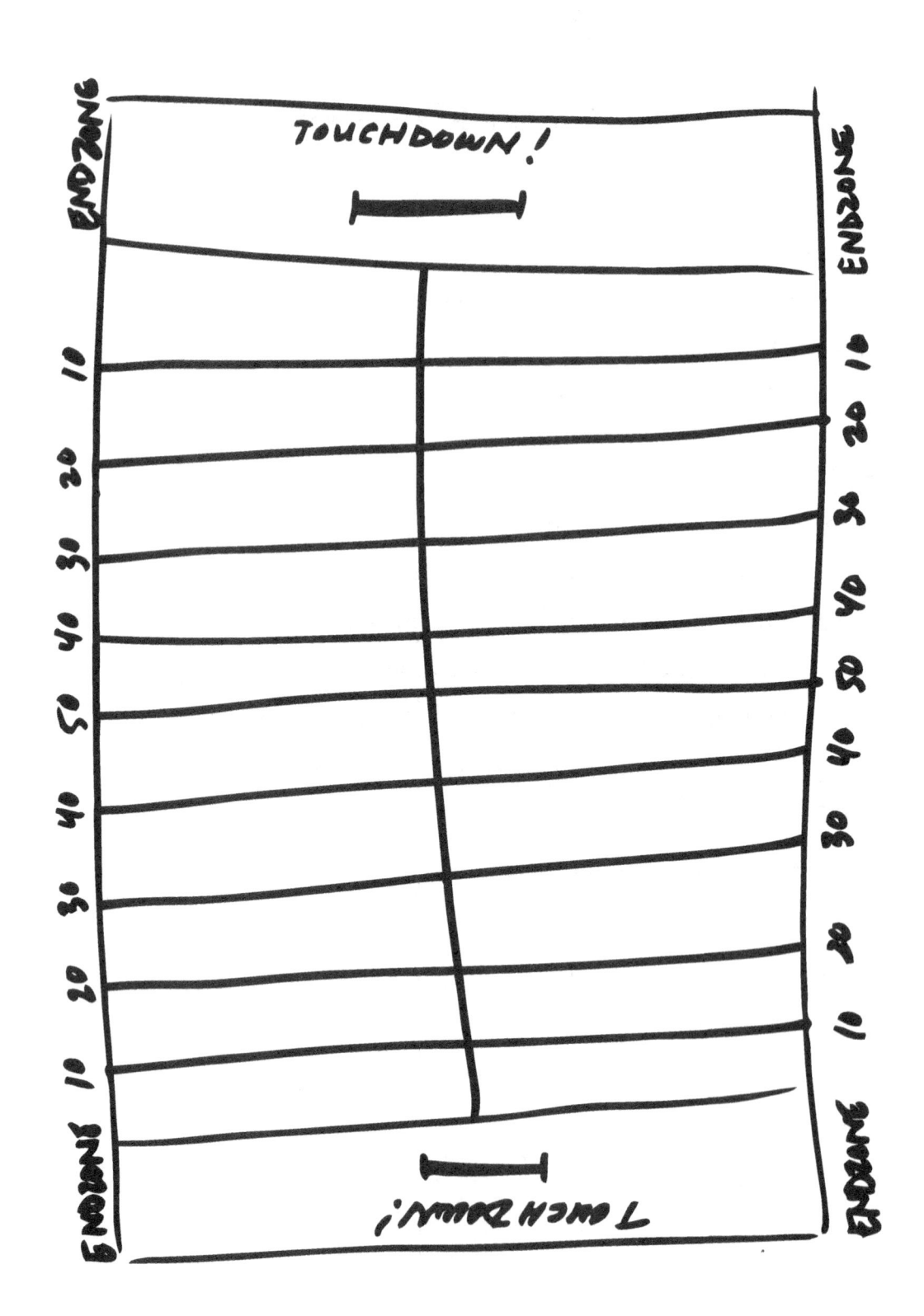

Bazooka Boys ★ Who Am I?

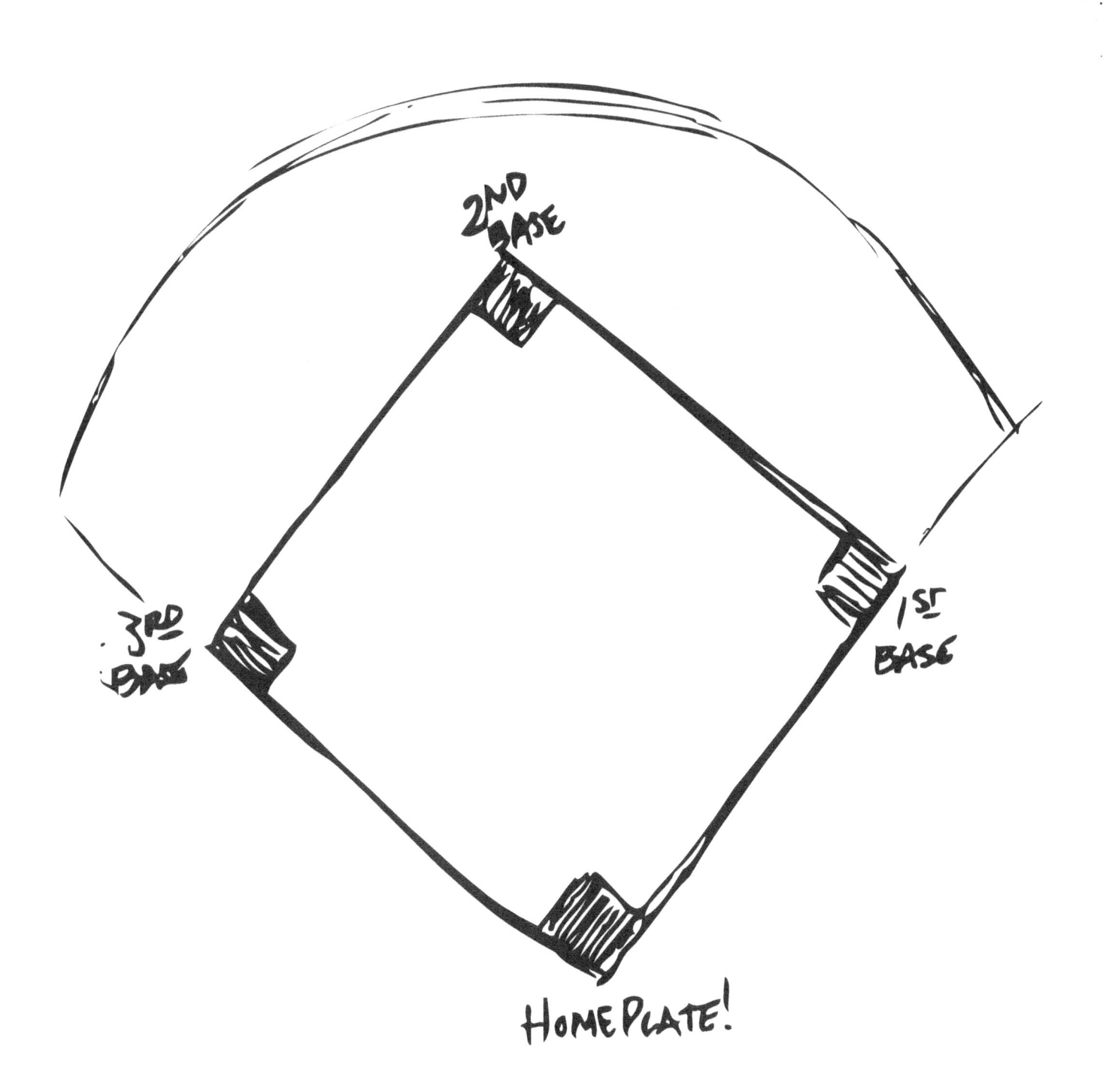

WEEK 4

2ND BASE

3RD BASE

1ST BASE

HOME PLATE!

Bazooka Boys ★ Who Am I?

WEEK 4

Bazooka Boys ★ Who Am I?

WHO AM I?

WEEK 5

WHY AM I HERE?

WHAT'S THE POINT?
God has a purpose for your life.

THEME VERSE

I know the plans I have in mind for you, declares the LORD; they are plans for peace, not disaster, to give you a future filled with hope.
—Jeremiah 29:11 (CEB)

RELATED BIBLE STORY

Jeremiah 1:1–9

Have you ever had a to-do list? Maybe your mom or dad has given you a list of things you need to do before you could go outside and play. Maybe your teacher has given you a list of things you need to work on before lunch time. Or maybe you just like to make lists for yourself. I love to make lists and then cross them out when I finish each item. It's a really good feeling to cross things off a list!

WHO KNEW?

Have you ever heard of a to-do list before? It's a list of things you need to get done. Sometimes other people make a to-do list **FOR** you. Sometimes, your parents might call it a "honey do list" because it sounds nicer to say, "Honey, could you please do this for me?" But it still means the same thing: "Hey! Get this done!"

Do you know that God has a to-do list for you? It's true! And it's not just a list for what you need to do today or tomorrow—He has a list of what He wants you to do **EVERY DAY OF YOUR WHOLE ENTIRE LIFE**! He has big plans for you! Jeremiah 29:11 says, "'*I know the plans I have in mind for you,' declares the LORD; 'they are plans for peace, not disaster, to give you a future filled with hope'*" (CEB).

You know what I think is just amazing? God lets you and I be part of His plans. I mean, He's **GOD**! If He wanted something done, He could just say the word and make anything happen. (Kind of like He did when He created the whole universe!) But instead, He lets us be His helpers! He gives us jobs to do and then gives us all the things we need to get the job done. I think that's pretty awesome.

God uses people to do His work on earth. He tells us in the Bible that we're to help take care of the people on earth. We're to help those who need help. We're to be kind and show the love of God to others. Most importantly, we're to tell other people about Jesus!

So, how do we know what's on our to-do list from God? Well, we know He has things He wants each of us to do, but MY list is going to look a lot different from **YOUR** list. Why? Because God gave each of us different things that we care about and are good at. The things that are unique about you are the things God wants you to use to get your to-do list done!

Cameron has always cared about other people. When he sees someone who's sad, he **HAS** to try and help them feel better. He always seems to know the right thing to say to encourage them. It just comes really easily for him.

It's no accident that Cameron cares about people. God made him that way! When He created him, He put gift of compassion inside him, which helps him notice other people's feelings and care about helping them. God gave Cameron that gift because He needed someone to make other people feel loved. So, God gave Cameron the gift of compassion and wrote in **SUPER HUGE** letters on Cameron's to-do list: "CARE FOR PEOPLE!"

Bennett couldn't be more different than Cameron. He is pretty shy around other people, but he **LOVES** to spend time alone in his room reading books and writing. He could write in his journal for hours every day! He loves to play Scrabble, do crosswords and word finds, and spend time doing **ANYTHING** that has to do with words.

You know why God created Bennett with a love for words? Because He wanted him to write things. Books, letters, poems, stories . . . all kinds of things! God's to-do list for Bennett is to tell people about God by using words. And God's plan for him isn't just to use words when he's a grown up! Oh no! He wants him to start using his amazing gift right now. Bennett writes awesome stories that he shares with his friends. God wants everyone to know how much He loves them, and Bennett is going to help Him get the word out.

Then there's Trevor. Trevor likes to be in charge. People seem to follow him and listen to the things he says. He likes making decisions and is always thinking of ways to make things better. Just like Bennett and Cameron, it's **NO** accident that Trevor is the way he is. You know why? Because God created him to be a **LEADER**. When He was creating him, He gave him the ability to inspire other people and help guide them. God needed someone who could direct other people to Him, so he wrote **"LEAD"** on Trevor's to-do list.

That's just a few examples! There are hundreds of ways God wants to use you. He has amazing things planned for you, and He's given you everything you need to do His plan for your life.

Sometimes you and I can feel like we don't have a to-do list from God. We're not sure why we're here. We don't feel very important. We haven't figured out what's on our list, so we just decide God doesn't want to use us. Sometimes, we even think God wants to use everyone **EXCEPT** us, but that's SO not true!

God has a plan for you! He'll show you the things He has planned for your life. You don't have to compare your list to anyone else's because God made a list **JUST** for you.

Sometimes we don't think we can really do what's on our list. We might feel scared or too small to do anything for God. We might wonder how in the world we could do something as important as telling other people about Jesus. But God promises to help us with every single thing He has planned for us.

Bazooka Boys ★ Who Am I?

There's a man in the Bible who wondered if he could really do everything that was on God's to-do list for his life. His name was Jeremiah. God came to him and said, *"Jeremiah, I am your Creator, and before you were born, I chose you to speak for me to the nations."* (Jeremiah 1:4–5, CEV).

Woah! Pretty big stuff. God showed Jeremiah what was on his list. In big ol' letters, Jeremiah's list said: "**SPEAKER**." God told him that even before he was born, He knew him and designed him with the ability to speak to other people about God!

Jeremiah wasn't so sure about this. He said, *"I'm not a good speaker, Lord, and I'm too young."* (Jeremiah 1:6, CEV). Just like many of us respond to God's list for us, Jeremiah had lots of reasons he thought He wasn't good enough to do what God had asked him to do.

But God said something really amazing to Jeremiah. He said, *"Don't say you are too young. If I tell you to go and speak to someone, then go! And when I tell you what to say, don't leave out a word! I promise to be with you and keep you safe, so don't be afraid."* (Jeremiah 1:7–9, CEV).

God tells Jeremiah he doesn't need to be afraid because He'll always be with him. He tells Jeremiah he shouldn't worry about the words he'll say because He would put them right in his mouth! God makes it very clear to Jeremiah that He has a plan for His life and that Jeremiah better get to it!

What do you think is on **YOUR** to-do list ? What are the gifts God has placed in you? How could you use those things to help share His love with the world?

Think about the things you love. What do you get excited about? Helping your Dad build things? Playing sports? Organizing things? Taking care of your little sister or brother? Reading? Being outdoors? It's no accident that you love the things you love. God created you that way to help you with your to-do list!

What about the things you're good at? Maybe you **LOVE** math class or science or music. Are you really good at cleaning your room or helping your Dad mow the grass? Maybe you are really good at the computer and you love to figure out all kinds of games and programs. It's no accident that you're good at the things you're good at. God created you that way to help you with your to-do list!

What about the things that really bother you? Maybe you get really upset when you see someone getting picked on. Maybe you hear stories about children who live in other countries and don't have enough food, and you just can't stop thinking about it. Do you find yourself concerned about the environment and taking care of the earth God gave us? Maybe you get really excited about buying Christmas gifts for kids who can't afford them every year. It's no accident that the things that bother you bother you! God created you that way to help you with your to-do list!

God is asking you to help Him. Before you were even born, He had a plan for your life. He wants you to help Him care for the people of the world. He's asking you to use the gifts He gave you to share His love. He wants the whole world to know about Him—and He's going to use YOU to do it. Pretty cool!

Closing Prayer: "Dear God, Thank You for having a plan for my life. I want to tell others about You by using all the gifts You have given me. Help me to know what to do and what to say. I give You my life to do anything You ask of me. Thanks for letting me be part of what You're doing. I love you. Amen."

DOODLE PAGE

LESSON 5

God has given you gifts—things that you're good at—just like a superhero has a special super power. One may be able to fly while another has super strength. Some can see through buildings and others can build super cool gadgets.

Write out what **YOUR** superpower would be if **YOU** were a superhero! (Keep in mind the special gifts that God has given **YOU**! Then draw how you would use your superpowers to help other people!

My Superpower: _____

Bazooka Boys ★ Who Am I?

ACTIVITY SHEET

WEEK 5

God gave us the things we're good at as a gift in order to complete our to-do lists! Circle your top three favorite things to do to figure out your spiritual gifts!

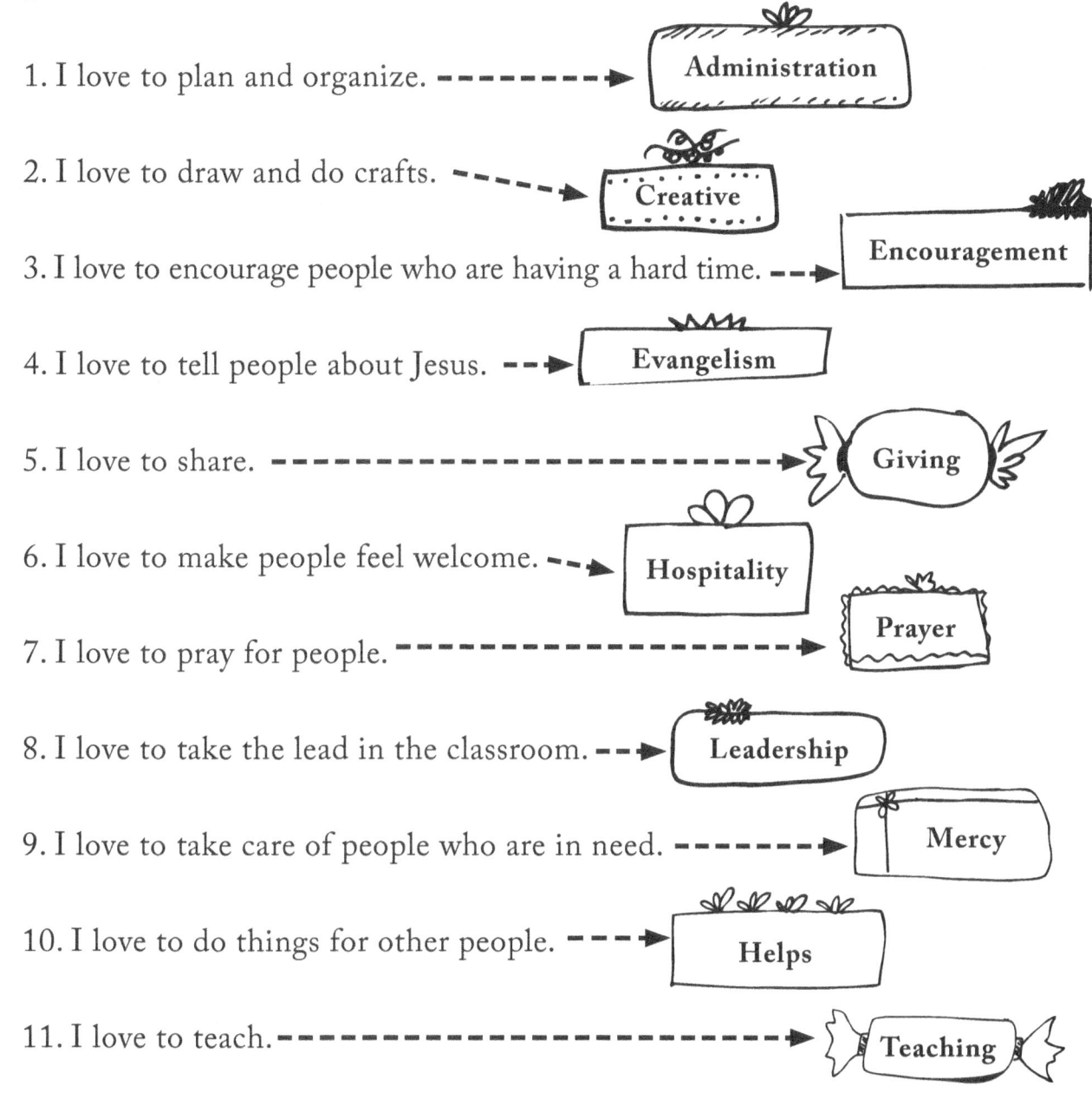

1. I love to plan and organize. → Administration

2. I love to draw and do crafts. → Creative

3. I love to encourage people who are having a hard time. → Encouragement

4. I love to tell people about Jesus. → Evangelism

5. I love to share. → Giving

6. I love to make people feel welcome. → Hospitality

7. I love to pray for people. → Prayer

8. I love to take the lead in the classroom. → Leadership

9. I love to take care of people who are in need. → Mercy

10. I love to do things for other people. → Helps

11. I love to teach. → Teaching

Spiritual Gifts Survey

Directions: Please rate yourself from 3 to 0. For each sentence, circle ONE number that represents you best.

Rating Scale: A score of 3 is something you do always, 2 is something you do most of the time, 1 is something you do once in a while, and 0 is something you've never done.

1. I like to organize.	3	2	1	0
2. I like to create things and make crafts.	3	2	1	0
3. I like to see the best in people.	3	2	1	0
4. I like to share Jesus with others.	3	2	1	0
5. I find it easy to trust God to answer my prayers.	3	2	1	0
6. I like to give my money to people in need.	3	2	1	0
7. I enjoy doing basic tasks for other people.	3	2	1	0
8. I like to make people feel welcome.	3	2	1	0
9. I like to execute plans.	3	2	1	0
10. I like to care for others.	3	2	1	0
11. I like to pray for other people.	3	2	1	0
12. I like to teach God's Word to others.	3	2	1	0
13. I am careful and can manage a lot of details.	3	2	1	0
14. I like to use my artistic skills in art, drama, music, dance, etc.	3	2	1	0
15. I like helping people feel better when they're sad or discouraged.	3	2	1	0
16. I am concerned for people who don't believe in God.	3	2	1	0

Bazooka Boys ★ Who Am I?

17. I believe God is always with me even when I'm having a hard time.

    3   2   1   0

18. I like to tithe to my church.   3   2   1   0

19. I like to help at my church.   3   2   1   0

20. I like to help new kids connect at school or church.

    3   2   1   0

21. I can motivate people to reach a goal.   3   2   1   0

22. I am patient with people who are having a hard time.

    3   2   1   0

23. I enjoy praying for long periods of time.   3   2   1   0

24. I like to study and share what I've learned with others

    3   2   1   0

25. I like to make and complete to-do lists.   3   2   1   0

26. I like to share God with others through art, music, or dance.

    3   2   1   0

27. I like to help people feel courageous when they are afraid.

    3   2   1   0

28. I am not afraid to share Jesus with others.   3   2   1   0

29. I trust God with everything I do.   3   2   1   0

30. I like to share what I have with my friends and family.

    3   2   1   0

31. I like to find things that need to be done and do them without being asked.

    3   2   1   0

32. I enjoy having friends over to my house.   3   2   1   0

33. I like to set up plans to achieve my goals.   3   2   1   0

34. I like to help people who have been ignored or rejected.

    3   2   1   0

WEEK 5

35. When I hear about something sad or a person in need, I pray right away.
3 2 1 0

36. I like to tell stories. 3 2 1 0

37. I like to help others get organized. 3 2 1 0

38. I like to use my imagination. 3 2 1 0

39. I like to encourage others who may be unsure if they believe in God.
3 2 1 0

40. I like to find opportunities to share my faith with people who don't believe in God. 3 2 1 0

41. I believe God will help me do great things. 3 2 1 0

42. I like to give my money to those in need rather than spend it on myself.
3 2 1 0

43. I like to help my family, friends, or teachers get things done.
3 2 1 0

44. I like to do whatever I can to make people feel like they belong.
3 2 1 0

45. I figure out what needs to be done and I do it. 3 2 1 0

46. I have great compassion for hurting people. 3 2 1 0

47. I feel honored when someone asks me to pray for them.
3 2 1 0

48. I find it easy to explain things to others. 3 2 1 0

Bazooka Boys ★ Who Am I?

Results:
- Write your score for each number (1–48) in the tables below.
- Add the numbers for each gift and put it in the total column.
- Circle the top three scores. These are your strongest gifts.

Administration	Creative Arts	Encouragment	Evangelism
1 _____	2 _____	3 _____	4 _____
13 _____	14 _____	15 _____	16 _____
25 _____	26 _____	27 _____	28 _____
37 _____	38 _____	39 _____	40 _____
Total _____	Total _____	Total _____	Total _____

Faith	Giving	Helps	Hospitality
5 _____	6 _____	7 _____	8 _____
17 _____	18 _____	19 _____	20 _____
29 _____	30 _____	31 _____	32 _____
41 _____	42 _____	43 _____	44 _____
Total _____	Total _____	Total _____	Total _____

Leadership	Mercy	Prayer	Teaching
9 _____	10 _____	11 _____	12 _____
21 _____	22 _____	23 _____	24 _____
33 _____	34 _____	35 _____	36 _____
45 _____	46 _____	47 _____	48 _____
Total _____	Total _____	Total _____	Total _____

My 3 Strongest Spiritual Gifts:

Gift 1 _____

Gift 2 _____

Gift 3 _____

WEEK 5

BAZOOKA BREAKDOWN

We all have to-do lists! Write some things that you have had to do in the last week or so (example: make your bed, clean your room…)

TO DO:

Bazooka Boys ★ Who Am I?

WEEK 5

God has a to-do list for your life too! Look at your activity sheets. What are some of the things that God has given you to help you do your "to-do list from Him?

Write out this verse three times and see if you can memorize it!

I know the plans I have in mind for you, declares the LORD; they are plans for peace, not disaster, to give you a future filled with hope.
—Jeremiah 29:11 (CEB)

Bazooka Boys ★ Who Am I?

BAZOOKA PROJECT

WEEK 5

MY TO-DO LIST BOOKMARK

Supplies:
- Cardstock
- Hole Punch
- Leather/Cord/String
- Markers/Crayons

Prep:
1. Copy the template onto cardstock
2. Cut out the bookmark

Directions:
1. Color the bookmark with crayons/markers.
2. Punch a hole at the top of the bookmark.
3. Thread leather/cord/string through the hole and tie at the top.
4. Write down your to-do list from God and keep it in your Bible or favorite book as a reminder to follow God's plan for your life!

MY "TO DO" LIST

MY "TO DO" LIST

MY "TO DO" LIST

MY "TO DO" LIST

WHO AM I?

WEEK 6

GOD-CONFIDENCE

What's the Point?

Our confidence isn't in what we can do, what other people think of us, or even what we think of ourselves. Our confidence is in God.

THEME VERSE

For you have been my hope, Sovereign LORD, my confidence since my youth.
—Psalm 71:5 (NIV)

RELATED BIBLE STORY

Philippians 3

Sam had a problem. His teacher had asked him to lead an afterschool book club and announced to the whole class that he would be in charge of the group—picking the books, organizing the meetings, and leading the discussion time. Sam **LOVED** to read, but the teacher was asking him to do something **WAY** different than just read a book! She was asking him to be in charge of something.

A million questions ran through his head. What if no one comes? What if no one likes my ideas? What if I don't know what to say? What if my hair looks silly that day and everyone is staring at me? What if I actually pass out from nervousness in front of everyone? Sam was not feeling very confident.

What is confidence? Confidence is believing you can do something. It's knowing that you can do anything. It's feeling strong and sure about yourself and your abilities. It's being okay with who you are and what you can do and holding your head up high.

What is Confidence?

The last thing Sam was feeling was confident. All he could think of were the reasons he couldn't do it. The more he thought about it, the more he doubted himself and just wanted to quit the whole thing altogether.

Have you ever felt really confident about something? Maybe you're really good at a certain thing and when you do it, you feel proud and strong inside. Maybe you feel confident when you step onto a soccer field. Maybe you feel confident when you're playing the piano. Maybe you feel confident when you're doing homework or taking a test.

What about times when you **HAVEN't** felt confident? I'm sure you can think of a few of those! When you have to try something new? When you have to do something that you're **NOt** very good at? When you are around new people and

WEEK 6

you're not sure what they're going to think of you? I know there are **LOTS** of moments when I don't feel very confident.

So, what's the key to being confident? What would you say if I told you that there was a way for you to feel confident no matter what you were doing, where you were doing it, or who was around? Can you imagine?

There **IS** a way for you to have confidence in every situation you face. There **IS** a way for you to feel strong in every job or task you find in your hands. And there **IS** a way to feel confident about who you are, what you look like, and your place on the earth.

How? By finding your confidence in God.

I know that might sound confusing. How can you find confidence in yourself by finding confidence in God? Well, when we give our lives to God, and we belong to Him, everything we say and do is wrapped up in Him.

Sam was asked to lead book club because God planned it for him! Because God planned it for him, God is going to help him do his very best. He's going to help him pick the right book. He's going to give him the words to say for the discussion time. He's going to give him ideas and direction. Knowing God will never let him down and has promised to help him no matter what he's doing should give Sam **GREAT** confidence! God **NEVER** messes up, and if He's going to help Sam, then Sam is going to do a great job!

The truth is, most of us feel confident in the wrong thing. We look to lots of different things to make us feel secure and strong, but most of those things end up leaving us **LESS** confident.

Let's talk about a few of them.

Many of us try to have

1. SELF-CONFIDENCE

Have you ever heard that word before? A lot of people talk about having self-confidence. Self-confidence is believing in yourself. Now, I bet you're wondering why in the world that would be a bad thing, right? It's not a bad thing. It's awesome to feel good about yourself and the things you're good at. God doesn't want you feeling bad about yourself. He's your biggest cheerleader. He wants you to be strong, confident, and secure.

But I'll tell you why self-confidence can be a tricky thing. Why does Sam feel good about himself when he's **READING** a book, but not when he has to lead a discussion about a book? Sam knows that he's good at reading. He's self-confident in his ability to read quickly and understand what he is reading, but he **DOESN'T** feel self-confident about his ability to lead a group.

It's a **GOOD** thing for Sam to be proud of his reading skills, but if that's the only way he's going to feel confident about himself, he's going to be pretty limited in what he feels good about! What about all the times he has to do things he's not super good at? What about the times when he has to try something new? Unfortunately, being confident in yourself only helps you feel good about a few things—the rest of the time you're probably going to feel awful.

There was a man in the Bible named Paul who learned to not be confident in the things he was good at. And man, oh man, was he good at a lot of things. He was a very successful man who had studied at the best schools, came from the best family, hung around with the most important people, and held a high position. There was a time when Paul didn't know God, and he was very proud and confident in all his abilities and strengths.

Bazooka Boys ★ Who Am I?

Then something amazing happened. Paul found Jesus. He had an incredible, life-changing encounter with God and became a great missionary who shared Jesus with countless people and even wrote a large part of the Bible!

Paul wrote these words in Philippians 3:3: "*We put no confidence in human effort, though I could have confidence in my own effort if anyone could.*" Paul learned that even though he was good at a lot of things, he couldn't put his confidence in himself. He had to keep his eyes on God.

I don't know about you, but I want to feel confident in **ALL** the areas of my life, not just the things I'm good at. When I keep my eyes on myself and what I am able to do, I usually feel overwhelmed and discouraged.

When I stop and look to God and His promise to help me with everything I ever need, I can walk into any situation with the confidence that God is going to help me. I remember what the Bible says in Philippians 4:13: "*I can do everything through Christ who strengthens me.*"

God wants us to rely on Him! When we begin to rely on ourselves, we miss a huge part of who God wants to be in our lives! He wants to be our helper. He wants us to always look to Him for strength and courage. When we feel like we can do it ourselves, we start to think we don't need God.

> "*We put no confidence in human effort, though I could have confidence in my own effort if anyone could.*"
> —Philippians 3:3

It's like my three-year-old daughter. She always says, "I do it myself!" Now, she **THINKS** she can do everything herself, but the truth is, she needs my help. I can teach her how to do new things and show her the right way. When she won't let me help her, she's missing out on a lot! When we start to be confident in our own abilities instead of relying on God, we're saying, "I do it myself!" We could do so much more and God could show us so many new and awesome things if we'd just let Him help us, but for many of us, our self-reliance makes us think we don't need His help.

We need to replace our self-confidence with a reliance on God. Self-confidence says, "I can do that!" but God-confidence says, "God will help me do that."

Another way that we find confidence in the wrong place is by trying to have

2. PEOPLE-CONFIDENCE

Keaton's parents were very encouraging. They were constantly telling him how strong and talented he was. They were always pointing out what a good job he had done on things, and how proud they were of him. He always felt confident around his family.

Then he met Mrs. Burkus, his second grade teacher. She was **NOT** encouraging. At all. She never told Keaton he was doing a good job. She always pointed out the ways Keaton could have done better. She didn't compliment him on his math test or tell him she appreciated his help with the lunch count every day.

Keaton felt **HORRIBLE** every time he had to walk into Mrs. Burkus' classroom. He hated being there. No matter how good he did on his work, he always felt like he wasn't doing a good job because Mrs. Burkus didn't encourage him.

Pretty soon, Keaton didn't just feel bad about himself in Mrs. Burkus's classroom, he felt bad about himself all the time. Why didn't his teacher like him? Why didn't she say nice things to him? He just couldn't help thinking that if Mrs. Burkus didn't like him, he must not be very likeable.

Has that ever happened to you? Maybe you don't have a Mrs. Burkus, but maybe you have someone else who hasn't been very nice to you and suddenly you find your confidence **GONE**. It's happened to me. I

Bazooka Boys ★ Who Am I?

have found myself feeling nervous and self-conscious about areas I used to feel really confident in because of something someone else said to me.

Do you know why that happened to me? Because I was trying to find confidence in other people. I felt good about myself when **THEY** felt good about me. I felt good about my abilities when **THEY** felt good about my abilities. If they were happy with me, then I was happy with myself. Yuck!

That's **NO** fun, and it's **NOT** the way God wants you to live your life. That's why He tells us to **ONLY** put our confidence in Him and **NOT** other people. Psalm 146:3 says, *"Don't put your confidence in powerful people."*

> *"Don't put your confidence in powerful people."* —Psalm 146:3

We're not supposed to look to other people to make us feel strong, secure, or confident. That's God's job, and we're not supposed to try and get anyone else to do God's job for Him.

When you're looking to other people to make you feel confident, you constantly have to be thinking about what would make **THEM** happy or what **THEY** would want you to say or do instead of wondering what would make **GOD** happy or what **GOD** wants you to do. The Bible says we aren't supposed to put pleasing other people above pleasing God. Galatians 1:10 says, *"Obviously, I'm not trying to win the approval of people, but of God. If pleasing people were my goal, I would not be Christ's servant."* I want to please God, don't you? We can't please Him if we're focused on pleasing other people.

When you feel nervous or insecure about something, ask yourself these questions: What does God think of me? Is what I'm doing making Him happy? Is this something He wants me to do? Remind yourself that if He asked you to do something, it's because He believes in you and is going to help you do the very best job you can. If God's happy with you, you can have all the confidence in the world despite what other people may think or say about you. Remember what Psalm 118:8 says: *"It is better to take refuge in the Lord, than to trust in humans"* (NIV).

Keaton had to realize he couldn't change Mrs. Burkus. But just because Mrs. Burkus wasn't encouraging him, it didn't mean she didn't like him or believe in him. **EVEN IF IT DID**, her opinion of him didn't matter because he knew God had made him smart and talented and believed in him. That was all Keaton needed.

It can be so easy to put our confidence in ourselves or try to find it in other people's opinions of us. But God wants you to find your confidence in **HIM**. Trust that He believes in you. Trust that He is always with you. Trust that He will give you the strength to do **ANYTHING** He asks of you.

I want to leave you today with a letter written by our good ol' buddy Paul. He wrote these words in 2 Thessalonians 2:15–17: "*So, friends, take a firm stand, feet on the ground and head high. Keep a tight grip on what you were taught, whether in personal conversation or by our letter. May Jesus himself and God our Father, who reached out in love and surprised you with gifts of unending help and confidence, put a fresh heart in you, invigorate your work, enliven your speech*" (MSG).

God believes in you. That's all the confidence you need.

Closing Prayer: "*Dear God, thank you for believing in me. Keep me from looking to find confidence in my own abilities or what other people think of me. Help me to find my confidence in You. Amen.*"

DOODLE PAGE

LESSON 6

God-confidence says, "God will help me do that!" In the space provided, draw a picture of yourself doing something you're afraid to do. With God-confidence you can do it!

For YOU have been my HOPE, sovereign Lord, my CONFIDENCE since my youth.
—Psalm 71:5 (NIV)

Bazooka Boys ★ Who Am I?

ACTIVITY SHEET

WEEK 6

You can always put your confidence in God and trust Him completely. Read each verse below and write the word TRUST in the blank spaces.

It is better to take refuge in the Lord, than to _____ in humans. —Psalm 118:8 (NIV)

When I am afraid, I put my _____ in you. —Psalm 56:3 (NIV)

We are confident of all this because of our great _____ in God through Christ. —2 Corinthians 3:4 (NLT)

But blessed is the one who _____ in the LORD, whose confidence is in Him. —Jeremiah 17:7 (NIV)

A verse about having God confidence is hidden in the puzzle below. To find it, cross out every other letter, starting with A. Write the remaining letters in the blanks at the bottom of the page.

A F P O G R B Y Q O H U D H L A R V O E K B M E F
E C N S M T Y J H L O S P T E V S G O H V D E P R
A E M I Z G U N Y L F O W R S D N M C Y T C R O Y
N L F W I S D K E R N P C H E B S Z I K N Y C P E
G M O Y A Y T O Q U W T C H A P G S J A K L D M

___ ___ ___ ___ ___ ___

___ , ___ ___ ,

___ ___ ___

___ ___ . ___ ___ 71:5

109

The key to confidence is to _____ _____ _____.

To find the answer to the question above,
- Look up each of the verses below in your Bible. (All verses NIV)
- Fill in the blank.
- Circle the first letter of the word you put in the blank to discover the key to confidence.

Do not put your _____ in princes, in human beings, who cannot save. —Psalm 146:3

It is better to take _____ in the Lord, than to trust in humans. —Psalm 118:8

Like a broken tooth or a lame foot is reliance on the _____ in a time of trouble. —Proverbs 25:19

For You have been my hope, _____ LORD, my confidence since my youth —Psalm 71:5

When I am afraid, I put my _____ in you. —Psalm 56:3

For it is we who are the circumcision, we who serve God by his Spirit, who boast _____ Christ Jesus, and who put no confidence in the flesh. —Philippians 3:3

Should _____ your piety be your confidence and your blameless ways your hope?. —Job 4:6

Such confidence we have through Christ before _____. —2 Corinthians 3:4

My heart, _____God, is steadfast; I will sing and make music. —Psalm 57:7

I can _____ all this through him who gives me strength. —Philippians 4:13

Bazooka Boys ★ Who Am I?

BAZOOKA BREAKDOWN

WEEK 6

What does is mean to be **CONFIDENT**? In the acrostic below, match the words that describe confidence with the letters provided.

Fierce

Not afraid

Determined

Excited

Take risks

Courageous

Overcoming

Independent

Never gives up

C _____
O _____
N _____
F _____
I _____
D _____
E _____
N _____
T _____

We discussed 2 things we sometimes put our confidence in that will eventually let us down. Write those two things in the small circles. *(hint: look back at the lesson if you need to.)*

Now, what should we put our confidence in instead? Write the answer next to the picture below.

Bazooka Boys ★ Who Am I?

WEEK 6

We should put our confidence in **GOD** because **HE IS STRONG** and will **NEVER LET US DOWN!**

Write out this verse three times and see if you can memorize it!

For you have been my hope, Sovereign LORD, my confidence since my youth.
—Psalm 71:5 (NIV)

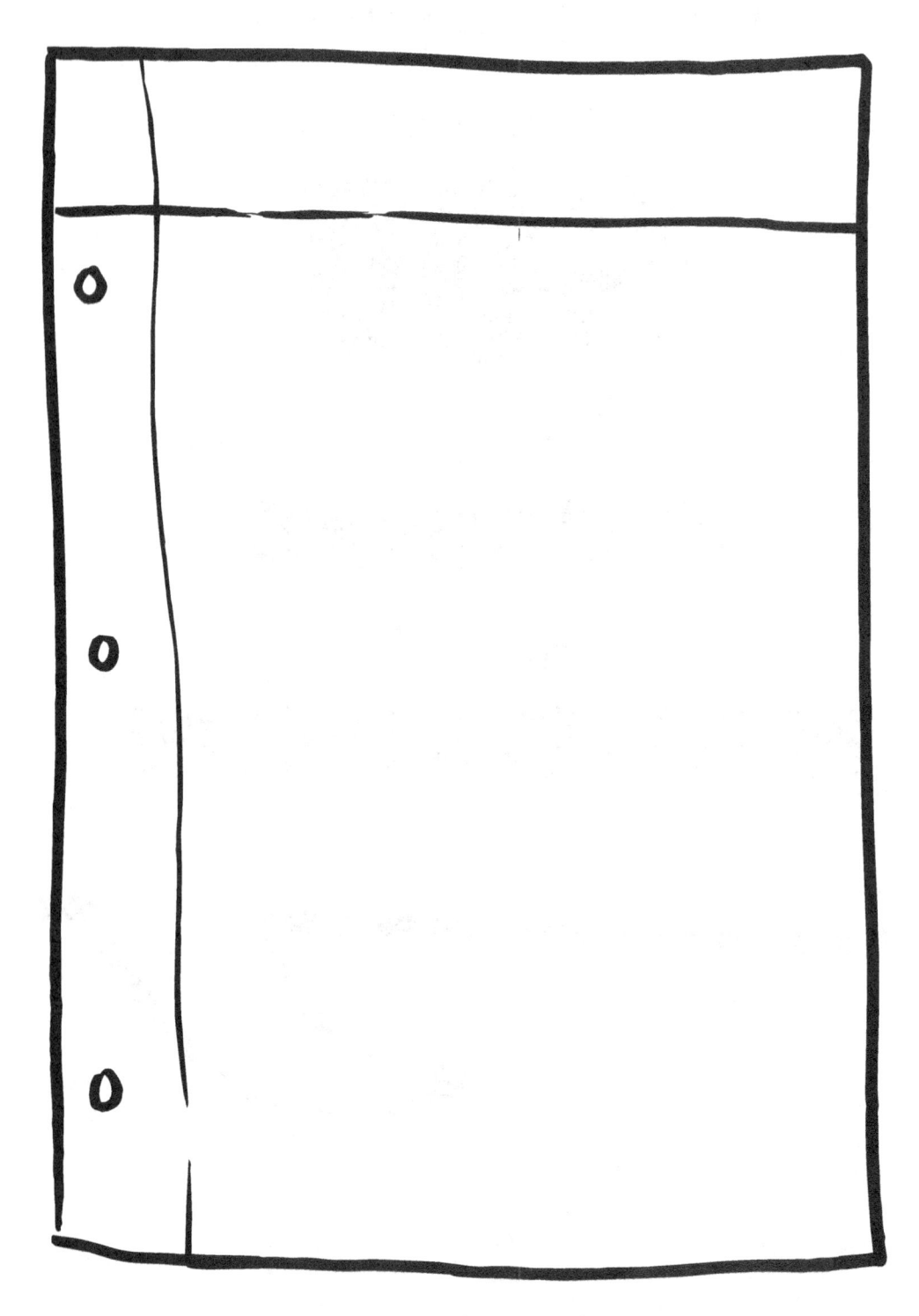

Bazooka Boys ★ Who Am I?

BAZOOKA PROJECT

GOD-CONFIDENCE JOUSTERS

Supplies:

- Pool Noodles
- Duct Tape
- Electrical Tape
- Serrated bread knife (for parent use only)

Directions:

1. Have your parent cut each pool noodle in half with the bread knife.
2. Wrap duct tape around approximately 4–5 in. of one end of each noodle.
3. Wrap the electrical tape around the bottom to make a handle.

Bazooka Boys ★ Who Am I?

WHO AM I?

WEEK 7

SO MUCH STUFF!

WHAT'S THE POINT?
God wants you to love Him more than your stuff.

THEME VERSE

For where your treasure is, there your heart will be also.
—Matthew 6:21 (NIV)

RELATED BIBLE STORY

Luke 18:18–23

Nathan was **NOT** looking forward to going back to school on Monday. It was the first day back after Christmas vacation, and he knew everyone was going to be talking about all the amazing gifts they got. "Oh my goodness! You got the brand new whatchamacallit and so-in-so? So did I! But I got one in every color so I could have **OPTIONS**!" New bikes, games, computers, toys—you name it, those kids got it. It's not like he wasn't happy for them, but every year the same thing would happen. Eventually, someone would ask him what HE got for Christmas.

That's when Nathan wanted to crawl under his desk and hide. His dad had been out of work for a really long time. Actually, Nathan couldn't remember a time when his dad **HAD** a job. He had been sick and it was just too difficult for him to work. His mom had a job, but it didn't pay very much money, and most of the money she made went to pay his dad's medical bills.

Christmas at Nathan's house just wasn't the same as his friends' Christmas. His parents would get him one small gift that usually didn't cost very much money. He was thankful for what he was given, but when he compared it to the piles of gifts everyone else from school got, he couldn't help but feel sad and embarrassed. Why couldn't his family have more money? And why couldn't he bear to tell anyone what was going on at home? He was so scared people would make fun of him because he didn't have much money.

Matthew was in a completely different situation. His family **DID** have a lot of money. He always had lots of presents under the Christmas tree, and if he wanted something, his parents usually bought it for him. All his friends loved to come to his house because of all the cool things he had in his room and all the awesome toys and games he had.

After a while, Matthew started feeling like his friends only wanted to come over because of his stuff. He didn't feel like they really cared about him. He wondered if people would still want to spend time with him if he didn't have fun things at his house. Why didn't people want to know him simply for who he was? Were people trying to be his friend just because of the stuff he had? He was so scared that people wouldn't like him if he didn't have much money.

Bazooka Boys ★ Who Am I?

WEEK 7

And then there's Ryan. Ryan's family wasn't really poor, but they weren't really rich either. He couldn't get everything he wanted, but his Mom and Dad were able to buy him lots of nice things. Most days, Ryan was pretty shy, but as soon as he got a cool toy or a new video game that he could show his friends, he suddenly felt more confident. When he had a new backpack or a new bike, it made him feel like people would notice him. He didn't feel quite as nervous when he had something new to show his friends.

The problem was that Ryan was starting to rely on **STUFF** to make him feel confident. Instead of being happy with who God made him to be, he was using **THINGS** to try and make himself feel confident. What would he do if suddenly he had to face a new situation without a new toy to help him feel sure of himself? What would he do if he had to let people see him without all the new flashy things to get attention? He was so scared that he would have to face the world without all his **STUFF**.

Have you ever felt bad because you wanted something but couldn't have it? Have you ever felt embarrassed because you didn't have a certain kind of clothes or a certain toy or game that all your friends had? Or maybe you have a lot of nice things and you find yourself getting caught up in all the STUFF in your life. You feel like people don't see you, just the cool things you have. Or maybe you're relying on your stuff to make you feel confident or likeable.

It's really, really easy to get caught up in our **STUFF**, isn't it?—the stuff we **HAVE** and the stuff we **DON'T HAVE**. It can feel like we're not as cool as other guys if we don't have the stuff they have. Or it can feel like people only like us for our stuff. And sometimes we can start to rely on our **STUFF** to make us feel good about ourselves instead of just being okay with who we are.

Believe it or not, the Bible talks a lot about **STUFF**. You might not actually find the word **STUFF** in the Bible, but the idea of money and things comes up **A LOT!** Jesus knew how big of a deal money and things could become in our lives.

WHO KNEW?
There are more verses in the Bible that talk about money than about love—over 1,000!

The problem with **STUFF** is that we can get **SO** wrapped up in the things we have and don't have that **STUFF** can become too important to us.

Matthew 6:21 tells us *"For where your treasure is, there your heart will be also."* (NIV). A treasure is something that's really important to you. It's the thing you spend the most time and energy thinking about. Our treasure is what's closest to our hearts. God wants our hearts to be His! He wants us to trust Him and love Him and think about Him, but when we become too concerned with our **STUFF**—when our **STUFF** becomes our treasure—our hearts belong to our **STUFF** instead of God.

There's a story in the Bible about a man whose heart was all tied up in his **STUFF** instead of God. He was a very rich and important man, and one day He came to Jesus and asked Him what he should do in order to be one of His followers. Jesus asked him a few questions and finally said, *"'Then there's only one thing left to do: Sell everything you own and give it away to the poor. You will have riches in heaven. Then come, follow Me.' This was the last thing the official expected to hear. He was very rich and became terribly sad. He was holding on tight to a lot of things and not about to let them go."* (Luke 18:22–23, MSG).

Why do you think Jesus asked the man to sell everything he had? Did Jesus want him to not have **ANY** money? I don't think so. I think Jesus knew this man's heart was all tied up in his **STUFF**, so He asked him to give it all up. Unfortunately, this man wouldn't let go of all the things he had. He loved his **STUFF** more than he loved God.

How can you make sure your heart isn't too tied up with your stuff?

1. BE CONTENT WITH YOUR STUFF.

Bazooka Boys ★ Who Am I?

Do you know what the word "content" means? It means being happy with the way things are. Someone who is content isn't worried about getting more things. They're okay with what they have. Being content means you don't spend a lot of time thinking about what you don't have or what you want to buy.

Scottie was **OBSESSED** with video games. He just loved getting new games to play. He would spend time on the computer looking at new games and he was always paying attention to the latest releases. The problem was the more he looked at all the new stuff he wanted to get, the more he started to **HATE** everything he already had! All his games seemed boring and old. He started to realize his obsession with new games meant he wasn't content with the games he had.

Hebrews 13:5 says, "*Don't be obsessed with getting more material things. Be relaxed with what you have.*" (MSG). God doesn't want you constantly thinking of all the **STUFF** you want to get. He wants you thinking about way more important things! When you start spending so much time thinking and asking for things, your heart gets more and more tied up in your stuff. Instead, God wants you to be thankful for the things you have! He wants you to have a grateful heart that's okay with the toys and clothes you have, thankful for things that you DO get, and not always worrying about what you **DON'T** have.

The second way you can make sure your heart isn't tied up with too much stuff is

2. KNOW THAT YOU ARE SO MUCH MORE THAN YOUR STUFF.

Sometimes we can feel like we have to have just the right clothes or just the right toys in order for people to want to be our friends. When we don't feel confident about ourselves, it's easy to feel like a new game or a new toy will make us more comfortable or likeable.

But you don't need that stuff! God made you amazing and cool and

DON'T WORRY ABOUT STUFF!!!

fun, and you can be confident in who He made you to be. If people only want to be your friend because of the things you have, they're not really your friends anyway!

When you start to feel like you want to show off something new to make people like you better, stop yourself. When you feel like you need to have something new so you won't feel nervous on the first day of school, remind yourself that God is with you and there's no need to be nervous. When you start relying on the things you have to make yourself feel better, take a minute and ask God to help you feel strong in Him and not in other things. Psalm 138:3 says, *"As soon as I pray, You answer me; You encourage me by giving me strength."* God is all you need. You don't need all that stuff!

The third way you can make sure your heart isn't tied up with too much stuff is

3. DON't WORRY ABOUt StUFF.

Bazooka Boys ★ Who Am I?

WEEK 7

It can be easy to think about all the stuff we want, but there are times in our lives when our thoughts about money and things are way bigger than just wanting more stuff. Maybe you're really worried about just having enough. Maybe your mom and dad are going through a hard time and your family just doesn't have much money at all. Maybe you want new things but you know that your family can't afford them and you feel kind of sad about that. Maybe you get teased at school because you don't have the same kind of clothes the other kids have.

Just because you're a kid doesn't mean you can't feel nervous and scared about not having enough money. It can be a really yucky feeling to be worried about having enough food or clothes. And feeling different from everyone because you can't afford certain clothes and toys is no fun at all.

But you know what? Jesus knew that you might feel worried about those things and He wrote some things in the Bible just for **YOU**! One of my favorite promises from God is found in Matthew 6:31–33. It says, *"So don't worry about these things, saying, 'What will we eat? What will we drink? What will we wear?' These things dominate the thoughts of unbelievers, but your heavenly Father already knows all your needs. Seek the Kingdom of God above all else, and live righteously, and He will give you everything you need."*

God has promised to always take care of you. You don't need to worry about food and clothes, because God will always provide for you. When you feel yourself starting to worry, remember that God will always take care of you. Always.

God cares about you so much. He loves to bless you with things. First and foremost, He wants you to love Him with all your heart. God wants you to love Him more than your **STUFF**.

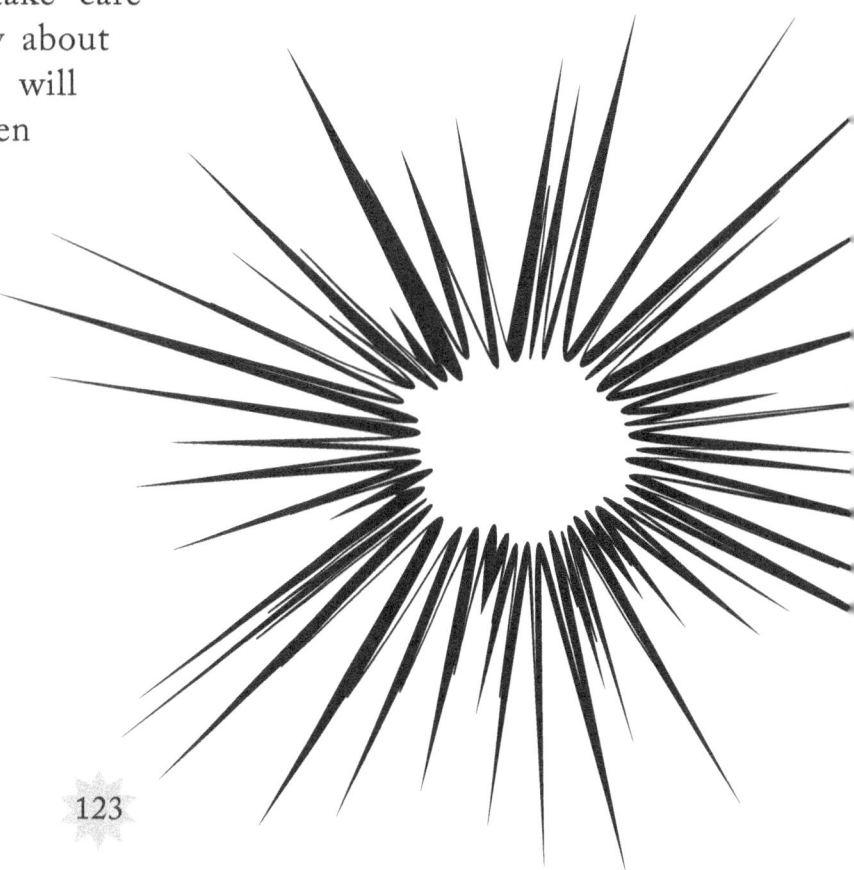

"Not that I was ever in need, for I have learned how to be content with whatever I have. I know how to live on almost nothing or with everything. I have learned the secret of living in every situation, whether it is with a full stomach or empty, with plenty or little. For I can do everything through Christ, who gives me strength."
—Philippians 4:11–13

Closing Prayer: *"God, I want my treasure to be found in You, not all my stuff. Help me to love You more than things. Show me how to be content with what I have, and remind me that You will always take care of me. Amen."*

DOODLE PAGE

LESSON 7

Matthew 6:21 says, *"For where your treasure is, there your heart will be also."* (NIV) Inside the heart, draw some of your favorite stuff. It can be things you have or things you would like to have. Over the top, write the word **GOD**. Remind yourself that it's okay to have stuff, but God must always be our treasure.

Bazooka Boys ★ Who Am I?

ACTIVITY SHEET

WEEK 7

Read each verse below and circle the word that should go in the blank. Go to your Bible and check your answers!

1. *For where your treasure is, there your _____ will be also* (Matthew 6:21, NIV).

    a. dog   b. God   c. heart

2. *Love the Lord your God with all your _____* (Deuteronomy 6:5, NIV).

    a. money   b. heart   c. cookies

3. *Don't be obsessed with getting more material things. Be _____ with what you have* (Hebrews 13:5, MSG).

    a. worried   b. relaxed   c. mad

4. *It says, "So don't _____ about these things, saying, 'What will we eat? What will we drink? What will we wear?'"* (Matthew 6:31–33, NLT).

    a. pout   b. ask God   c. worry

5. *Not that I was ever in need, for I have learned how to be content with whatever I have. I know how to live on almost nothing or with everything. I have learned the secret of living in every situation, whether it is with a full stomach or empty, with plenty or little. For I can do _____ through Christ, who gives me strength* (Philippians 4:11–13, NLT).

    a. nothing   b. everything   c. most things

6. *Watch out! Be on your guard against all kinds of _____ ; a man's life does not consist in the abundance of his possessions* (Luke 12:15, NIV).

    a. greed   b. spiders   c. money

7. *Think about the things of _____, not the things of earth* (Colossians 3:2, NLT).

        a. LEGOs   b. heaven   c. love

8. *And God will generously provide for all you _____. Then you will always have everything you need and plenty left other to share with others* (2 Corinthians 9:8, NLT).

        a. want   b. desire   c. need

BAZOOKA BREAKDOWN

A treasure is something valuable. Something that is **REALLY** important to you. In the treasure chest below, write a few things that you **TREASURE**.

Now look at the things that you listed. Are there a lot of **THINGS**? Is there a lot of **STUFF**? The Bible says that we shouldn't let our hearts treasure **ANYTHING** more than God. Is there anything listed above that you've let become more important to you than it should be?

Draw a circle around that thing and ask God to help you not to treasure it more than you treasure Him! Now, write in **BIG, AWESOME** letters the name **JESUS** over your treasure chest! Remember that God should be what we treasure the most!

Write out the following verse three times and see if you can memorize it!

"For where your treasure is, there your heart will be also."
—Matthew 6:21 (NIV)

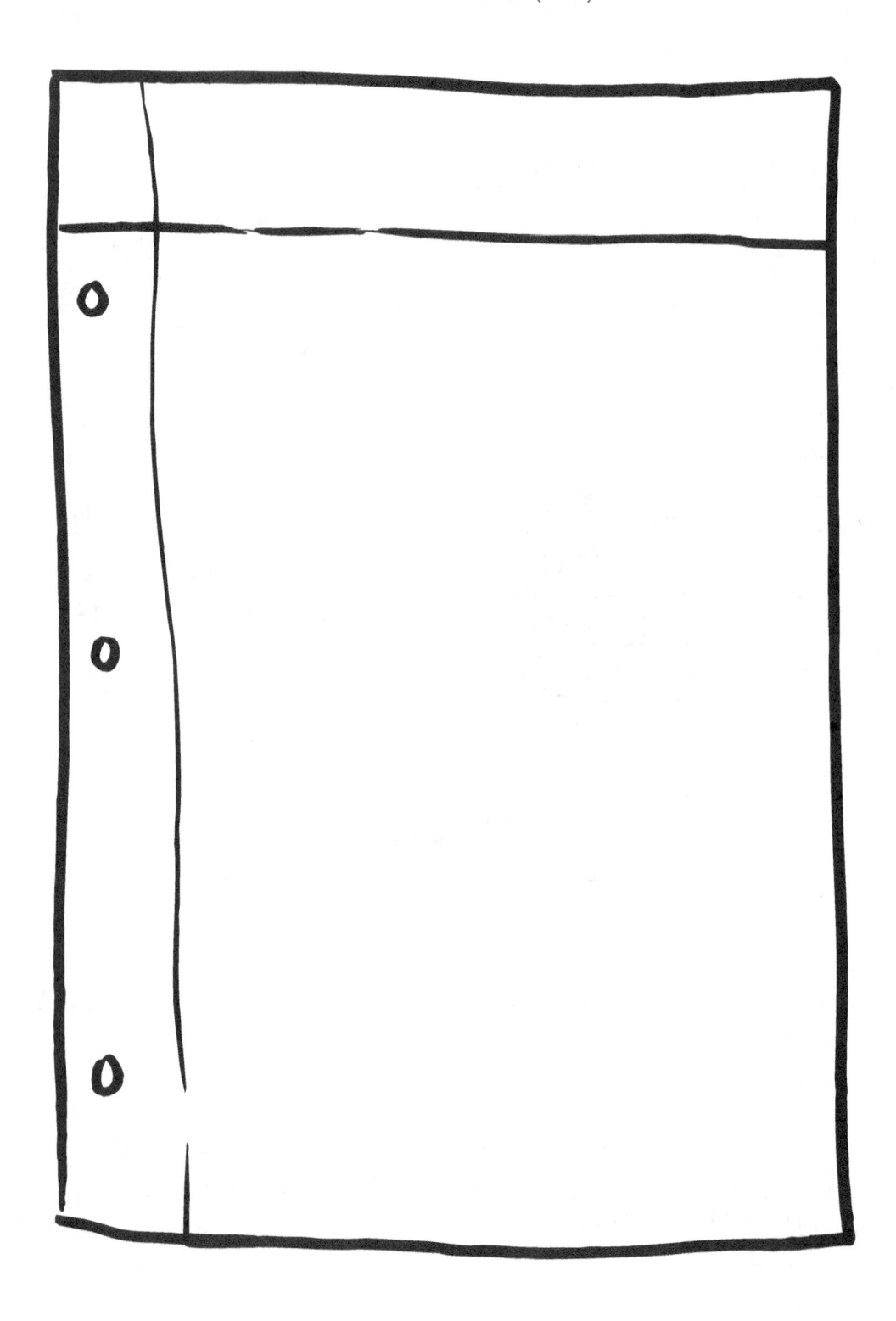

Bazooka Boys ★ Who Am I?

BAZOOKA PROJECT

WEEK 7

GOD HAS MY HEART TREASURE ROCKS

Supplies:
- Bowl
- Baking soda
- Water
- Food coloring or washable watercolors
- Treasures (Oriental Trading is a great site to purchase small crosses, angels, and other small treasures)
- Shallow dish (optional)
- Vinegar (optional)
- Spray bottle (optional)

Directions:
1. Add some baking soda to a bowl.
2. Add a few drops of food coloring.
3. Slowly add water and mix.
4. Slowly add more water until the mixture is damp and mold-able, but not too wet. (If you accidently add too much water, just add a touch more baking soda.)
5. Mold the baking soda dough into balls.
6. Take a baking soda ball to mold and hide a treasure inside.
7. Lay the baking soda rocks on a cookie sheet or flat surface to dry. Drying will take approximately 24 hours.
8. Hide the rocks and go on a treasure hunt.
9. Break open the rocks to find the treasures:
    - Place the treasure rocks in a shallow dish

- Pour vinegar into the spray bottle
- Spray the treasure rocks with vinegar
- The more you spray the rocks, the more they'll fizz and eventually break apart to reveal the treasure.
- You can also put the treasure rocks directly into a bowl of vinegar and watch them erupt.

WHO AM I?

WEEK 8

COURAGE

What's the Point?

God gives me courage to face tough situations, take a stand against wrong words or actions, and helps me do things bigger than I can ever imagine.

THEME VERSE

*Be strong and **courageous**! Do not be afraid or discouraged. For the Lord your God is with you wherever you go.*
—Joshua 1:9

RELATED BIBLE STORY

Deuteronomy 31:1–8

I am scared to death of grasshoppers. Yup, grasshoppers. I know that seems like a silly thing to be scared of, but I just can't seem to help it! They're so weird looking and they jump on you out of nowhere. One time I came inside after working in my yard and my daughter said to me, "There's something on your back." Just then, this H-U-G-E grasshopper jumped off my back right onto the kitchen counter. I screamed and jumped and screamed and ran around in circles and then screamed a little more until it finally jumped into the sink and washed down the drain. My kids still tease me about it all the time.

We all have silly little things we're afraid of (like grasshoppers), but there are lots of other **REALLY** scary things we have to face every day. Maybe you are super scared of walking into a classroom where you don't know anybody. Maybe you're afraid of having to be away from your mom and dad sometimes. Maybe you're afraid of the dark or of getting lost.

Being scared is no fun. Some people want to cry when they're scared. Other people get angry when they're scared. Some kids want to hide behind their mom or dad and some of us just don't know what to do!

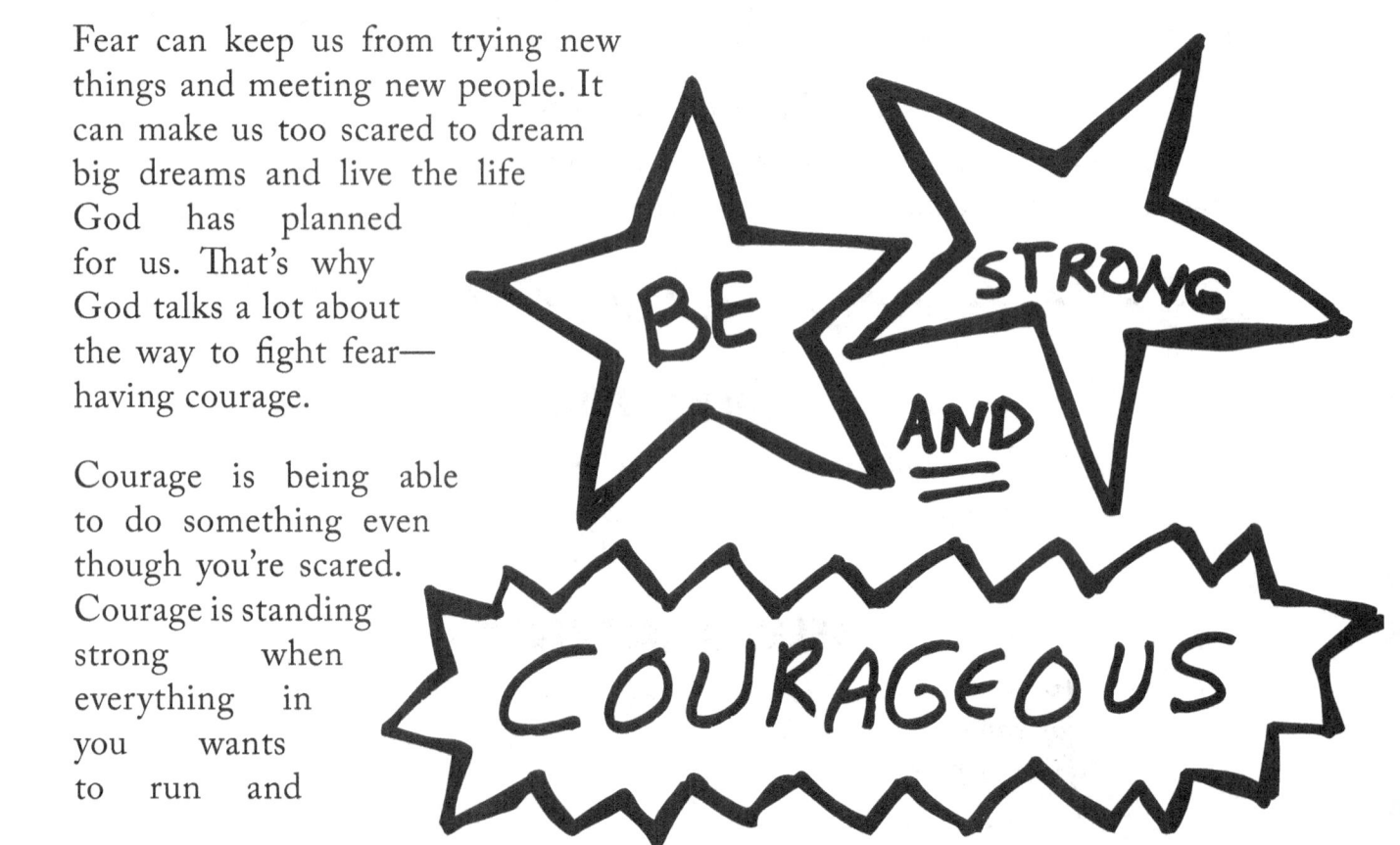

Fear can keep us from trying new things and meeting new people. It can make us too scared to dream big dreams and live the life God has planned for us. That's why God talks a lot about the way to fight fear—having courage.

Courage is being able to do something even though you're scared. Courage is standing strong when everything in you wants to run and

BE STRONG AND COURAGEOUS

Bazooka Boys ★ Who Am I?

WEEK 8

POP!

hide. Courage is doing the right thing even when the wrong thing seems easier. Courage fights fear.

God wants you to be courageous. He wants you to face your fears and stand strong. The Bible is full of stories about people overcoming things they were really, really afraid of. In each story, God helped the person get past their fears and go on to do really amazing things.

One of those stories was about a guy named Joshua. When God led the children of Israel out of Egypt, Moses was the leader chosen to guide the people. Joshua was one of his helpers.

When Moses was 120 years old (yikes!) he stood in front of the people and made a speech. He said, *"I am now 120 years old, and I am no longer able to lead you. The Lord has told me, 'You will not cross the Jordan River.' But the Lord God himself will cross over ahead of you. He will destroy the nations living there, and you will take possession of the land. Joshua will lead you across the river, just as the Lord promised."* (Deuteronomy 31:2–3).

Um, what? Can you imagine what Joshua must have been thinking in that moment—Me?! I am going to lead the people now…into a land of people who want to kill us?—Can you imagine how scared he must have been? Not only did he have to take over for, you know, **MOSES** (only the greatest leader ever!) he had to lead the people into a new land that had all kinds of people who hated them and wanted to kill them. Not the easiest job!

I'm sure Joshua felt a **LOT** of things, but more than anything else, I bet he felt **SCARED**. I bet his stomach got all tied up in knots and his hands started to shake. I bet his mind started listing all the reasons there was **NO WAY** he could do the job. I bet he was **FULL** of fear.

But then Moses says something very important to Joshua: *"Be strong and courageous! For you will lead these people into the land that the Lord swore to their ancestors He would give them…Do not be afraid or discouraged, for the Lord will personally go ahead of you. He will be with you; He will neither fail you or abandon you."* (Deuteronomy 31:7–8).

BE BRAVE.

Isn't that cool? It's like God knew exactly how Joshua would be feeling in that moment and He had Moses speak these words to help Joshua fight his fear. God knew Joshua would be scared. He knew he would feel overwhelmed. He knew Joshua would doubt his abilities.

But God made a promise to Joshua in that moment. He told him He would be with him. He said He would never fail or abandon him. God told Joshua to stand and be courageous because HE was going to be with him always.

God makes the exact same promise to you and me. You don't have to be afraid of **ANYTHING** because God will always be with you and help you. He will never fail you. He will never leave you.

What are some ways you can be **COURAGEOUS**? How can you fight fear and get past some of the things you're afraid of?

Well, first of all, you must

1. BE BRAVE.

What does it mean to be brave? It means that when you feel afraid to do something, instead of quitting or running away, you do it anyway.

Ethan was going through a hard time. He was afraid of being away from his mom and dad. For some reason, he just didn't want to go to friends' houses anymore or sleep over at his grandma's. Whenever he tried to go somewhere without his parents, he got a horrible feeling and got so nervous that he just stayed home.

His mom and dad prayed with him that God would help him overcome his fear. He even began to memorize Psalm 118:6: *"The Lord is for me, so I will*

Bazooka Boys ★ Who Am I?

STAND UP

have no fear." He knew God would be with him whenever he went somewhere, even if his mom and dad weren't there.

One day a friend asked Ethan to come to his house for a play date. At first, Ethan felt the old familiar scary feeling, and he was ready to just stay home, but he realized he needed to fight his fear and be brave. Even though he felt a little nervous, he took a deep breath and went over to his friend's house. Once he got there, he had SO much fun! He was so glad he didn't let his fear stop him from spending time with his friend.

The next time a friend asked him to come over, he was still a little afraid, but it was easier. Again, he took a deep breath, reminded himself that God was always with him, and decided to be brave. After a few times, he didn't even feel scared anymore!

Sometimes we have to do things even though we're a little nervous. Sometimes we have to be brave and face our fears. Maybe you're afraid of the dark and need to ask God to help you be brave. Maybe you're afraid to trying out for a team and God is asking you to take a deep breath and try out anyway. Being brave means you don't let your fear stop you from doing something. And Jesus will **ALWAYS** help you be brave.

Another way you can be courageous is to

2. STAND UP.

Have you ever been in a situation where someone was saying or doing something you knew was wrong? Have you ever been around someone who was telling you to do something you didn't want to do, but you felt really nervous about saying no? Have you ever had a friend treat you badly, but you were too scared to stick up for yourself?

Sometimes the best way to show courage is standing up. Sometimes you have to stand up to people who are doing something wrong and tell them to stop. Sometimes you have to speak up and say "no," even if it means that person might make fun of you or not want to be your friend anymore. And sometimes, you have to stand up to someone who is treating you poorly and tell them to stop.

Stephen was in a tough situation. His friend Tyler hadn't studied for his math test, and during lunch, he leaned over and asked Stephen if he could copy his answers during the test. Stephen knew it was wrong and he **REALLY** didn't want to cheat, but he was afraid of what Tyler would say or do if he didn't help him. At first, he nodded his head okay, but the moment he did it, he knew in his heart that it wasn't the right thing.

"So we can say with confidence, 'the Lord is my helper, so I will have no fear. What can mere people do to me?'"
—Hebrews 13:6

Everything in him was super scared to stand up to Tyler, but Stephen knew it was the right thing to do. So, he mustered up all the courage he could and said, "I'm sorry, Tyler, but I just can't do that. I wouldn't feel right about cheating." Tyler gave him a dirty look and walked away angry. Stephen definitely didn't feel good about the fact that Tyler was mad at him, but he knew in his heart that he had made the right decision. It took a lot of courage to stand up to him, but Stephen was so thankful that he did.

Whenever you have to face another person and you're nervous about standing up to them, remember this verse. Hebrews 13:6 says, *"So we can say with confidence, 'the Lord is my helper, so I will have no fear. What can mere people do to me?'"* Remember that people are just people! It's way more important to do the right thing even if it means someone might be mad at you for a while. God is with you and will give you the courage to stand up for what it right.

Bazooka Boys ★ Who Am I?

The last way you can be courageous is to

3. TAKE A CHANCE.

Alan had a dream. He loved to play baseball and dreamed about being a professional baseball player when he grew up. He practiced hard every day, and his coach was always encouraging him. Then one day his coach told him he thought he should transfer to another team, one for more advanced players.

Alan was thankful for the opportunity, but he was terrified of going to a team where he didn't know anyone at all. In addition to that, his new coaches were going to be much harder on him and push him more than the coach he had now. Everything about it made him excited, and everything about it made him nervous.

Should he stay where he was and not have to face the fear of trying something new? Or should he take a chance and see just how far he could go? Alan knew that the new team wouldn't be easy, but it would help him live his dream.

After praying about it, he decided to go for it. He knew God would be with him and help him face anything difficult. No matter what, he could count on the fact that God would be with him. The more he thought about it, maybe God wanted to use him to share Jesus with the boys and coaches on his new team. Not only could he learn more about baseball, he could also be a light to those who didn't know Him. No matter how scared he was, he knew that helping God show His love to the world was something he wanted to do.

God will put dreams in your heart. **BIG** dreams. Sometimes those dreams can seem way bigger than anything you could ever do on your own. Some people look at the size of their dreams and just get scared and discouraged and give up. They let their fear keep them from trying something new.

But God wants to help you do big things for Him! Ephesians 3:20 says, "*God can do anything, you know—far more than you could ever imagine or guess or request in your wildest dreams!*" (MSG). God wants to use you to do things bigger than you can even imagine!

Sometimes it's going to feel pretty scary, but if you let your fear keep you from stepping into what God has for you, you're going to miss out on some really great stuff. Instead, fight your fear and look to God to give you courage. He'll help you do great things!

We all have things we're scared of, but we don't have to let our fear keep us from doing things, standing up for ourselves, and dreaming big. With God on our side, we have nothing to fear.

Closing Prayer: *"Dear God, help me to be brave. Give me courage when I feel afraid. Help me to stand up for the right thing. And help me to dream big for You. Amen."*

DOODLE PAGE

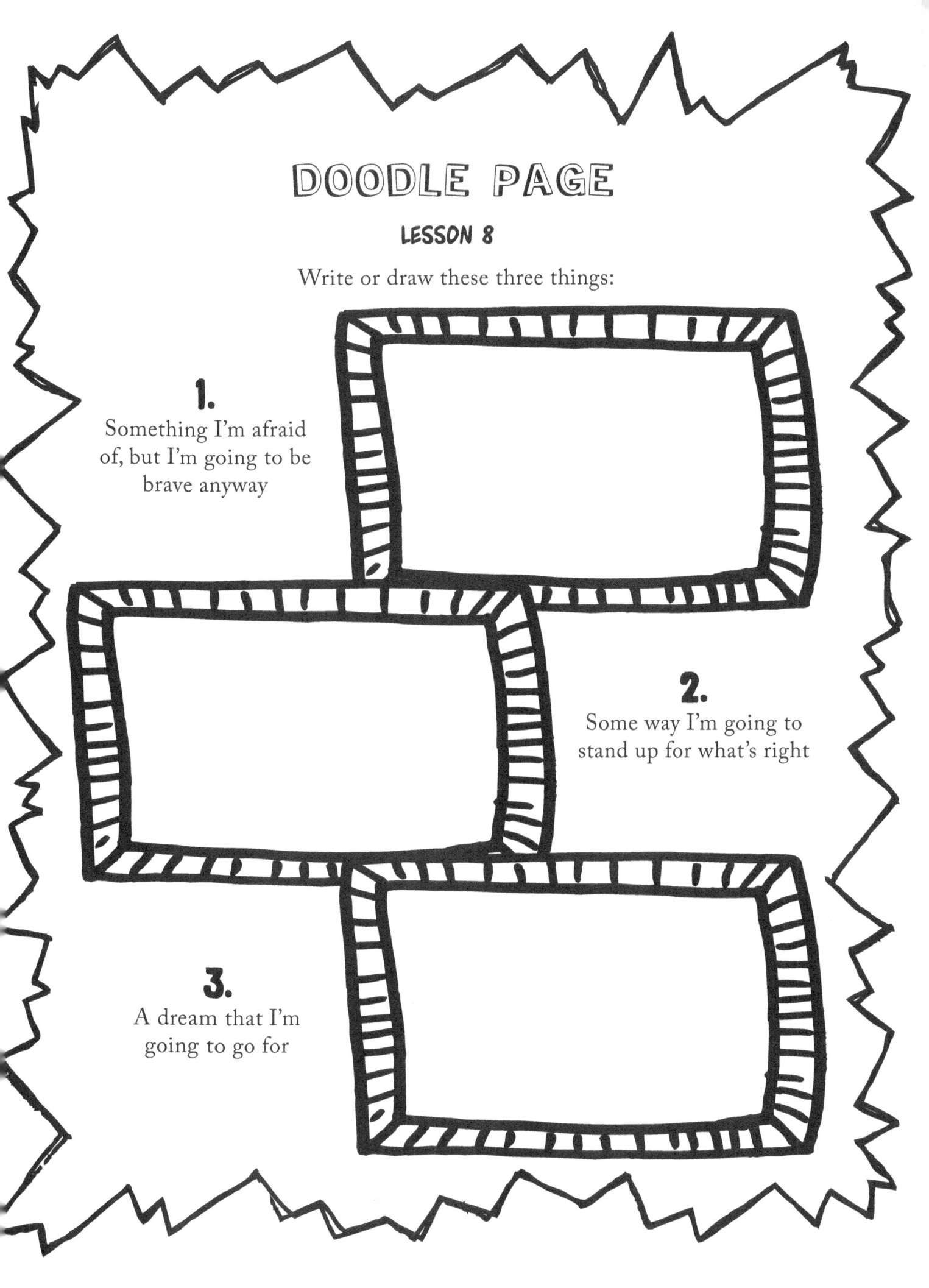

LESSON 8

Write or draw these three things:

1. Something I'm afraid of, but I'm going to be brave anyway

2. Some way I'm going to stand up for what's right

3. A dream that I'm going to go for

Bazooka Boys ★ Who Am I?

ACTIVITY SHEET

WEEK 8

You don't have to be afraid of ANYTHING because God will always be with you and help you. He will never fail you. He will never leave you.

The verses below talk about having courage. Read each verse and write the word COURAGEOUS in the blank spaces.

So be strong and _____! Do not be afraid and do not panic before them. For the Lord your God will personally go ahead of you. He will neither fail you nor abandon you. (Deuteronomy 31:6, NLT).

This is my command—be strong and _____! Do not be afraid or discouraged. For the Lord your God is with you wherever you go. (Joshua 1:9, NLT).

Be on guard. Stand firm in the faith. Be _____. Be strong. (1 Corinthians 16:13, NLT).

Being brave means you **DON'T** let your fear stop you from doing something, and Jesus will **ALWAYS** help you be brave. Read each verse and write the word **FEAR** in the blank spaces.

*So we can say with confidence, "The Lord is my helper, so I will have **NO** _____. What can mere people do to me?"* (Hebrews 13:6, NLT).

*Yes, you came when I called; You told me, "Do **NOt** _____."* (Lamentations 3:57, NLT).

*For God has **NOT** given us a spirit of _____ and timidity, but of power, love, and self-discipline.* (2 Timothy 1:7, NLT).

Cross out the Js, Qs, Ls, and Ps to find a message from God about courage!

PQBLJEJJPOLQNJJQGPQLJUQLJJAQQPRLPLD.
PQJJSQPLLJTQLLAPJPNQLQJDPLPLFJIPPRQ JQQMPQLILL
NQLPQTJHLLEJLJJFPJLAQIPPJTQH.
LPBQE JJCOQLUJRLLAPJQGQLLEJOPPUJLS.
PPLBQEJSPPTQRJLOQNJJLPG.
1JCLOPPRQJILLNPTLQHLJIPPAQLNPS:PQ1LJ6:Q1P3

_____

_____

_____

_____

Unscramble the letters to find a message from God about courage!

So be orngst ___ ___ ___ ___ ___ ___ and

eruocusoag ___ ___ ___ ___ ___ ___ ___ ___ ___ ___ ! And do not be

fdriaa ___ ___ ___ ___ ___ ___ and do not

npaci ___ ___ ___ ___ ___

beorfe ___ ___ ___ ___ ___ ___

hmte ___ ___ ___ ___. For the Lord your

odG ___ ___ ___ will personally go

Bazooka Boys ★ Who Am I?

haaed ___ ___ ___ ___ ___

oyofu ___ ___ ___ ___ ___. He will neither

ilfa ___ ___ ___ ___ you nor

aondanb ___ ___ ___ ___ ___ ___ ___

oyu ___ ___ ___.

ouermDnyteo ___ ___ ___ ___ ___ ___ ___ ___ ___ ___ 31:6 (NLT)

WEEK 8

145

BAZOOKA BREAKDOWN

Being **COURAGEOUS** means that you do something even thought you are scared. Color the badge of below and write in your name.

_____

is

Courageous

Bazooka Boys ★ Who Am I?

WEEK 8

God told Joshua to be courageous because He would always be with him. Think of a situation where you need to show courage. Draw a picture of yourself in the situation and remember that God will help you be **BRAVE!**

Write out the following verse three times and see if you can memorize it!

Be strong and courageous! Do not be afraid or discouraged. For the Lord your God is with you wherever you go. —Joshua 1:9

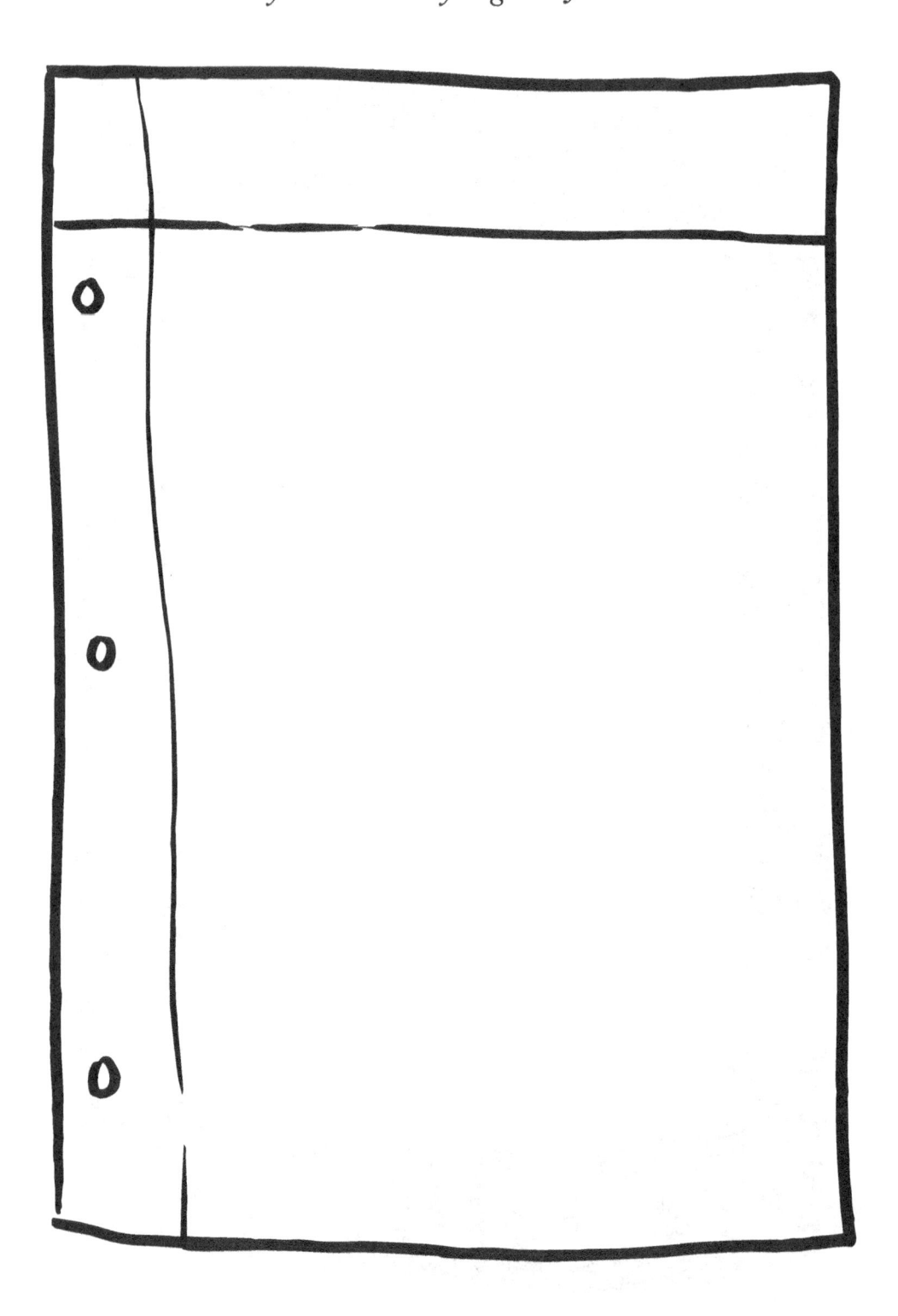

Bazooka Boys ★ Who Am I?

BAZOOKA PROJECT

WEEK 8

GOD'S COUPON BOOK

Supplies:
- Colored cardstock for coupon cover
- White cardstock for coupons
- Markers/crayons
- Stapler

Prep
1. Copy God's Coupon Book cover template onto colored cardstock.
2. Cut out each coupon cover.
3. Copy the coupon templates onto white cardstock.

Directions:
1. Cut out the coupons.
2. Decorate the coupon cover and coupons with crayons and/or markers.
3. Complete the coupons with your goals on bravery, standing up for what is right and your dreams.
4. Staple the cover and coupons together on the left side to create a booklet.

Templates:
1. God's Coupon Book – Cover
2. God's Coupon Book – Coupons

GOD'S COUPON BOOK

GOD'S COUPON BOOK

GOD'S COUPON BOOK

Good for unlimited amounts of
BRAVERY!

What _____

When _____

The Lord is for me, so I will have no fear. – Psalm 118:6

Good for unlimited amounts of
SELF-CONFIDENCE
to stand up for what is right!

To Who or For What _____

When _____

So we can say with confidence, "The Lord is my helper, so I will have no fear. What can mere people do to me?" – Hebrews 13:6

Good for unlimited amounts of
COURAGE
to accomplish your wildest dreams!

What _____

When _____

God can do anything, you know – far more than you could ever imagine or guess or request in your wildest dreams! – Ephesians 3:20 MSG